ELLY TWINEYO-KAMUGISHA

WHY AFRICA FAILS

THE CASE FOR GROWTH BEFORE DEMOCRACY

TAFELBERG

Tafelberg,
an imprint of NB Publishers,
40 Heerengracht, Cape Town, 8000
www.tafelberg.com

Cover by Michiel Botha
Cover photographs by Tim Chesney and Aldon Scott McLeod
Text design by Nazli Jacobs
Typeset in ATVeljovic

Printed and bound by Paarl Media Paarl,
Jan van Riebeeck Drive, Paarl, South Africa

First edition, first printing 2012
ISBN: 978-0-624-05536-5
E-ISBN: 978-0-624-05795-6

Contents

Preface

Historians usually recount what happened. Political scientists link history to the political management of society. Sociologists explain the underlying role of culture, family and history, etc., in society. Economists produce models and theories, and make assumptions about situations and how they impact on society. And economic historians portray economic growth and development, but from a historical perspective. Although I cannot claim to conform to any of these disciplines, I have followed, worked on and observed the challenges that sub-Saharan Africa faces as it rethinks its future.

I have written this book from the perspective of my personal experience of more than 20 years as a practitioner in the field of development. However, I am also guided by theoretical work in the fields of international business, international trade, development economics and political economy. I have had the privilege of discussing issues that confront African countries with international leaders, development practitioners, politicians, ordinary people, academics and students. And through discussions, observations and reading, I have come to one conclusion: colonialism is no longer a viable excuse for Africa's dismal performance in the global economic arena.

I believe that the solution to Africa's economic woes will not come from heaven. Instead, the solution will be the result of home-grown soul-searching and critical planning and commitment to work for prosperity – although it will take a long time to yield tangible results. In my view, 25 years will be sufficient for Africa to develop from the last to the first world. To achieve this feat, however, Africa will require courageous leaders, committed men and women who have a vision to steer the ship in the right direction. And, in addition, if sustainable rapid growth and high levels of income are to be achieved, Africans of all walks of life will have to work harder, but in smarter ways. As noted earlier, economic salvation will not come from heaven. It is through strategic thinking and smart, but hard, work that the developed economies have attained economic success. Their policies were tailored to suit specific challenges and aspirations.

Acronyms

ACP	African, Caribbean and Pacific Group of States
AfBD	African Development Bank
AGOA	African Growth and Opportunities Act
ANC	African National Congress
AU	African Union
BDP	Botswana Democratic Party
CBO	community-based organisation
CET	common external tariff
CIA	Central Intelligence Agency
COMESA	Common Market for Eastern and Southern Africa
CPA	Cotonou Partnership Agreement
CRB	credit reference bureau
DRC	Democratic Republic of Congo
EAC	East African Community
EC	European Commission
ECCAS	Economic Community of Central African States
ECOWAS	Economic Community of West Africa
EPA	Economic Partnership Agreements
EU	European Union
FDI	foreign direct investment
GDP	Gross Domestic Product
HIV/AIDS	human immunodeficiency virus/acquired immune deficiency syndrome
IDA	International Development Assistance

ILO	International Labour Organisation
IMF	International Monetary Fund
INGO	international non-governmental organisation
LDC	least developed country
LRA	Lord's Resistance Army
MDG	Millennium Development Goal
MFI	microfinance institution
NATO	North Atlantic Treaty Organisation
NGO	non-governmental organisation
OAU	Organisation of African Unity
PPP	public–private partnership
REC	regional economic communities
SADC	Southern African Development Community
UN	United Nations
UNCTAD	United Nations Conference on Trade and Development
UNECA	UN Economic Commission for Africa
UNESCO	United Nations Educational, Scientific and Cultural Organisation
UPE	Universal Primary Education
UPPET	Universal Part-Primary Education and Training
WHO	World Health Organisation
WTO	World Trade Organisation

Introduction

Soon after gaining their political independence – several of them in the 1950s and 1960s – many African nations embarked on a struggle for economic independence. Fifty years down the road, the struggle is yet to deliver meaningful results. Millions of Africans still live in dire poverty; many lives have been claimed by curable diseases; many breadwinners have been maimed in wars; and others are unemployed. In turn, their dependants have been deprived of education and healthcare, among other basic necessities.

In tandem with the continent's economic plight, many African states have failed infrastructure, and some depend on food aid. Although the economic emancipation struggle has been fraught with immense challenges, I, personally, do not buy into the repeated argument that colonialism is the main cause of Africa's current economic woes. I believe that the continent's plight is attributable to maladministration by its leaders. Many African nations have suffered long spells of poor leadership, dictatorship and gross corruption.

As explained earlier, this book is the result of my personal experiences and observation. Over the past two decades, I have represented Uganda – officially and later unofficially – at several development and trade engagements worldwide. I have interacted with bureaucrats and ordinary people from almost every part of the world. I have visited the rich and the poor, and seen how good policies can transform once feeble economies into great indus-trialised and stable nation states. I have interacted with officials from countries that were once poor but are now economically buoyant, thanks to good policies and leadership. Their countries achieved this as a result of enabling macroeconomic environments and government support. They pulled their scarce resources to-gether. And sooner than they had expected, these countries were on the path to economic freedom. However, I have also seen econ-omies crumble under the weight of bad regimes.

In this book, I argue that despite the effects of the colonial pro-ject (some Africans argue that the colonial experiment is yet to end), Africa should accept that its present malaise is largely due to its own mistakes: greed, poor policies and bad leadership. African countries must soul-search and find internal solutions to its prob-lems instead of relying on Europe, Asia and the US. Although most African leaders continue to extend the begging bowl to Western administrations, there is nothing to write home about what they have achieved in their endeavours. In a nutshell, aid has not been useful in terms of enhancing economic growth for African nations. Free things can never build nations, period. Over the past couple of decades, much foreign aid that has been extended to various African countries has been squandered by officials in govern-ment. And the activities of non-governmental organisations are not a panacea for development. In my opinion, we need an aid exit strategy. Although I agree with Zambian-born economist Dambisa Moyo (2009) that the entire aid system ought to be dis-banded, I do believe the last aid packages should be spent on en-hancing trade infrastructure to open up international markets.

My other humble plea is that rich nations should allow free trade to blossom. This would be a meaningful alternative to aid, upon which Africa has grown dependent. The role of African lead-ers would then revolve round stemming corruption, building in-frastructure, creating enabling business environments, marketing their countries, attracting investors and adding value to locally processed goods and services.

It is worth noting that in spite of the economic difficulties faced by Africa, the continent is nonetheless not a 'basket case', as often reported by the Western media. Most of their documentaries, press photos and stories give a false impression, namely that Africa is a continuing cycle of slums, squalor and poverty. There are, however, many positive stories – on governance, education and industrial growth, etc. – to report in various parts of Africa. And if these were accorded some decent air time or column space in the international media, several young Africans would be inspired to work harder.

Lastly, this book focuses on sub-Saharan Africa. It deliberately leaves out Arab Africa. The discovery of oil resources and their planning strategies have put the Arab African states in a different economic league from sub-Saharan Africa. And although they are yet to achieve their desired levels of economic development and good governance, they are nonetheless in better shape economically than their counterparts in sub-Saharan Africa.

Colonialism and the slave trade: Their impact on African economies

The slave trade robbed Africa of its strongest. Often, homesteads that had been raided were also razed. The strong were taken and, in most cases, the weak – women and children – were killed. There is no doubt that this affected African economies. The economic scars left by slavery remained visible long after African countries attained independence.

The questions we have long avoided asking ourselves as Africans are, were only the Europeans to blame for the slave trade? What about the Arab slave traders? And what about the African chiefs and kings who sold fellow Africans into slavery?

The Europeans needed labour and raw materials, and they came to Africa to obtain them. They worked out arrangements with African kings, chiefs and other rulers.[1] These rulers captured and sold their kith and kin either to the Arabs (who later sold them to the Europeans) or directly to the Europeans. In cases where rulers participated in selling their own people or those captured from less powerful neighbours, it is reasonable to say that these rulers betrayed their own. They sold them to buyers, who later turned them into slaves. We should also remember that these rulers[2] had domestic slaves whom they regarded as personal possessions, and saw no difference between slavery, whether it be on African or European soil. There has been a lot of silence surrounding these African betrayers. International fora and media continue to lay the blame on the white race as the only perpetrators of slavery.

We have to accept the reality that, in most cases, there was a willing seller (an African ruler) and a willing buyer (the whites or Arabs). The slave trade was commerce, an exchange via a transaction. Sadly, the transaction was the sale of Africans as slaves. It is also true that at times slave traders sailed to Africa to hunt for slaves, captured them and took them without paying.

The external slave trade took place across the Sahara, the Red Sea, the Indian Ocean and the Atlantic. In some countries, slavery benefited Arabs, especially in the case of those slaves who were traded via the Red Sea and trans-Saharan routes. This book does not concern itself with enumerating the various slave trades. However, we can conclude that the slave trade, unfortunate as it was, involved players other than just white Europeans.

The European colonial powers ruled most of sub-Saharan Africa from 1885 to the 1960s (although some countries, such as Zimbabwe, Mozambique and Angola gained their independence later). Consequently, many sub-Saharan African nations, in terms of their historical, political and economic development, are still in their infancy as independent states, and are still heavily influenced by their colonial heritage. Ghana, the first sub-Saharan African country to secure its independence from Britain in 1957, celebrated its 50th anniversary of independence in 2007.

The boundaries and names of African countries were not created by Africans. With the exception of Ethiopia, Liberia (thus named because it became the land of freed slaves) and Sierra Leone (also a land of freed slaves), the names and boundaries of African states were coined by European imperial powers during the 1884 Berlin Conference.[3] This forum was hosted by Otto von Bismarck, the chancellor of Germany, at the request of Portugal. Critically, this partitioning of Africa did not consider the importance of ethnic and religious aspects of the people. And not a single African was party to this parcelling out of the continent. Consequently, colonisation separated families and communities,

16

and people were forced to belong to two, or at times more, different countries.[4] For example, today, Rwanda's mainly ethnic Tutsis
live in Tanzania, Burundi, Uganda and the Democratic Republic
of Congo (DRC) instead of their own homeland, Rwanda. This
considerably affected the wealth creation effort of the affected
ethnic groups and undermined relationships that were an important ingredient of wealth accumulation.

The colonialists used a three-pronged approach.

Besides their military might (the gun), they also came under
the guise of spreading religion, and their third strategy was the
use of African collaborators. In Uganda, for example, the kings of
the Buganda Kingdom (the Kabaka),[5] who inhabited the central
region, were viewed as collaborators (Sejjakka, 2004).[6]

The colonial economies had reached a higher level of industrial
development and had markets. They also had revenue from taxes,
as well as other sources.

However, they needed raw materials and labour. Some writers
assert that the kind of institutions that were established by the
European colonialists for the purpose of either protecting private property or extracting rents transformed some prosperous
countries of the 16th century into the poorest economies of today
(Acemoglu et al. 2002).

Often, we have ignored the historical significance of the colonisation of Egypt by Arabs. In Greek, Egypt means the 'black land'.
Indeed, some African leaders assert that the original inhabitants
of Egypt, who built the pyramids, were black, not Arabs. According to Ugandan President Yoweri Museveni,[7] ancient Egyptians,
like the Somalis, were part of the ancient African peoples. They
were Cushites – part of the Nilo-Saharan group of peoples and
languages. Some of their words are even to be found in modern
Bantu dialects.

Colonialism and religion

Colonisation brought with it religion. In Africa, the two predominant religions are Christianity and Islam, both of which were introduced by the colonialists. The indigenous African religions were demonised and today they are regarded as backward and barbaric – forms of witchcraft.

There is a lot of politics associated with religion, but it is not appropriate to compare them all here. Suffice to say that religions are meant for the good of humanity, whether they are traditional African, Christianity or Islam, and they are important to their believers. We can say, however, that the colonial religions changed the way of life for Africans and, in the process, their art of survival. In Uganda the King of Buganda, Basamula Mwanga II, ordered the killing of his subjects who disobeyed his orders and converted to Christianity.

In the opinion of those who converted to Christianity, the king talked of in the Bible was superior to Mwanga. Many places that Africans have visited include places of pilgrimage associated with the imported religions – Jerusalem, Mecca, Rome and Canterbury, for example.

Colonialism and African economies

Most Africans who escaped being sold or forced into slavery in foreign lands worked in mines prospecting for minerals or were engaged in subsistence agriculture.

Decades later, when the colonialists introduced plantations of cotton, tea, coffee and cocoa, among others cash crops, Africans were forced to produce these commodities for the European and American markets. And for their sweat, they were paid a pittance. However, those African rulers who refused to collaborate with the colonial masters had their kingdoms decimated.[8]

According to Nunn (2003), during the period 1400–1900, no fewer than 12 million slaves from Africa were shipped abroad via the transatlantic route alone. Patrick Manning (1990) says that the effect of the slave trade was that by 1850, Africa's population was only half of what it would have been had slavery not taken place. And these estimates do not take into account people who were killed during the raids or those who perished due to lack of support once their senior family members and breadwinners had been taken as slaves. As human capital (labour) is a factor of production, the slave trade severely reduced labour capacity in Africa during that period, thereby hampering the rate of wealth accumulation and sustained economic growth.

Colonisation: No longer an excuse for Africa's current poor economic performance

The first sub-Saharan countries to achieve independence from European colonisation and imperialism were Ghana (1957) from the British, and Guinea (1958) from the French. These countries were followed by 15 others in 1960 alone. Zimbabwe gained its independence in 1980, and, more recently, South Africa achieved a democratic dispensation when it got rid of apartheid in 1994. Eventually all the African countries attained independence. Ethiopia and Liberia were never colonised.

I do not intend to analyse the history of what happened before independence. This sad story has already been told by historians. My intention, instead, is to critically diagnose the problems Africa currently faces and focus on finding practical remedies. It is worth mentioning, however, that colonisation did not take place only in Africa. While King Leopold of Belgium was ruling Zaire (now the DRC), Indonesia was being governed by a Dutch king. It was then known as the Dutch East Indies.

Before examining the underlying factors of Africa's economic failure and poverty, I wish to make it clear that, generally, Africa itself is to blame for its lack of growth and appalling levels of poverty. Africa's major handicap has never been (and will never be) lack of growth, but lack of sustained rapid growth. Its growth has been erratic. Africa's major challenge is its failure to sustain per capita income growth over a span of generations. Consequently, the majority of sub-Saharan Africans,[1] remain poor, sick and unemployed.

Using examples of developed countries we find that for a country to develop (and, therefore, for the number of those living in abject poverty to decline), it needs to sustain per capita income growth over a number of generations. Take the example of the United States. It has managed to grow its economy at an average of 1.5 per cent per year since 1860. Its average income per capita stands at $40 000. In sub-Saharan Africa, most countries have failed to achieve and sustain economic growth – with the exception of Botswana, which enjoyed growth at an annual rate of 6.8 per cent between 1986 and 2001, achieved by pursuing sound market friendly policies, and Uganda. Between 1987 and 2010, Uganda managed to sustain per capita income growth of around 2.5 per cent. This is impressive even by global standards. However, Uganda is yet to eradicate poverty, although the number of people living under the national poverty line fell from 56 per cent in 1992 to 31 per cent in 2006. This effort is laudable in light of the fact that the proportion of people living in extreme poverty in sub-Saharan Africa was 51 per cent in 2005.[2]

At the time of writing this book, there were still people in Uganda who had not benefited from this growth, and many others became unemployed during this period. What is important to help reduce poverty in society is not rapid growth alone, but also attaining high income levels. Nonetheless, by 2011, a Ugandan middle class had emerged and was growing. As an indicator, access to telephones rose from 62 000 to around 11 million over 20 years. In Uganda's capital, Kampala, and other towns, more shopping malls, arcades and leisure centres graced the skyline in the same period. More industries were built than ever before. However, the fertility rate stood at more than 7 per cent and population growth at 3.3 per cent annually.

One thing that Botswana and Uganda had in common, at the time of writing, was that both countries had market-friendly economic policies. This was one of the factors that stimulated and sustained their economic growth. But whereas Uganda was struggling to market and promote hides and skins in their primary form, Botswana had already penetrated the European Union (EU) market, had a profitable beef export trade and was looking for more customers. Uganda, which has large herds of cattle, was exporting tanned hides and skins to the EU while Botswana exported not only hides and skins but also quality meat.

The following sections examine the various internal factors that account for Africa's economic failure.

African leaders since independence

In the post-independence era, Africa has been cursed with selfish and unpatriotic leaders. There is only a very small number of iconic leaders from Africa's liberation era: Nelson Mandela of South Africa, Mwalimu Julius Nyerere of Tanzania, Kwame Nkrumah of Ghana and Patrice Lumumba of the Democratic Republic of Congo (DRC) remained patriotic to the letter. The rest had no vision for their countries. They were more interested in plundering and terrorising their own people. Most postcolonial leaders became looters, murderers, tribalists and mercenaries.

Eurocentric and Afrocentric historians, scholars and writers have different views of these four great leaders. The latter praise and recognise their contribution to Africa's independence and efforts at African unity, whereas the former claim that they were undemocratic. This book will maintain that these leaders did do something for Africa. This book also suggests that democracy evolves gradually; it experiences pitfalls before eventually becoming a reality. The United Kingdom seems to have followed a continuous path to democracy, but other countries were not so lucky. The process of democratisation is not smooth. African leaders after independence have suffered for two main reasons: they inherited a system of colonialism with its related subjugation and they had never experienced democracy before. And those African leaders whose countries were supported by the former Soviet Union faced the challenge that the socialist system was not viewed by capitalist or 'free-market' economies as democratic.

What did these leaders do for Africa?

Nelson Mandela is one of the world's most respected great leaders. He spent 27 years in prison on Robben Island, yet when he became president, as most whites of the apartheid administration had feared, he pursued a policy of peace and reconciliation. In 1994, he became the first black president of South Africa under the African National Congress (ANC), ruled for only one term and left office in 1999. He was awarded the Nobel Peace Prize in 1993. His charisma, sense of humour and lack of bitterness over his harsh treatment helped South Africa end apartheid and prevented the genocide of minority whites. When Mandela decided to negotiate with the apartheid regime, ANC leader Walter Sisulu, who had no trust in the apartheid regime, had differing views over such negotiations. Mandela insisted and his party finally agreed. And he negotiated successfully with the apartheid administration. Mandela agreed to negotiate with President de Klerk, and South Africa finally went to the polls.[3]

Mwalimu Julius Kambarage Nyerere[4] led Tanzania to independence after negotiating with Zanzibar's Abeid Karume. He was president from 1964 to 1985. Besides lacking professionals, such as teachers, engineers and doctors, Tanzania also lacked a unifying language. Through the help of opinion, cultural and religious leaders, Nyerere popularised Swahili as the national language. Fortunately, most people could speak and understand Swahili, irrespective of their level of education.

And courtesy of its national unity and pan-Africanist leader, Tanzania helped several countries to successfully oust their colonial masters. The toughest of these struggles was against apartheid in South Africa, and Nyerere was one of the most outspoken voices in the struggle against apartheid. Nyerere supported and promoted the independence movements in the region, and helped Uganda get rid of its notorious dictator, Idi Amin.

Realising that Tanzania had no money after independence but had resources in the form of land, Nyerere embraced a back-to-land policy for food security and economic growth. His aim was self-reliance through what was an essentially egalitarian policy. He established the Ujamaa[5] villages – a 'villagisation' programme. This programme became the cornerstone of Tanzania's rural transformation and development through collective production and distribution (from each according to his ability, to each according to his needs), as well as the facilitation of social-service delivery and development infrastructure. As a result, Tanzania has better roads than its immediate East African neighbours. Nyerere's Ujamaa villages programme and policies have been viewed as socialist. However, one should remember that during that period most African leaders preferred socialism to capitalism, arguing that African communities were socially oriented: working in farms as groups, building houses as a group, feasting together as a group and solving family problems as a group. So what is more important is not Nyerere's political ideology but what he did for his country and Africa as a whole. He established a culture of negotiation, as opposed to war between Tanganyika and Zanzibar. (Tanzania comprises Tanganyika and Zanzibar Island.) He also introduced stringent standards of integrity and ethical behaviour. During his time, Tanzania's politicians and civil servants were not as corrupt as its East African neighbours, Kenya and Uganda.

Nyerere developed the notion of African unity. However, unlike Nkrumah of Ghana and Touré of Guinea, he advocated a gradual approach to African unity. He argued that, like the gradual process of attaining independence, continental unity should also be established via a process. His view was that the first step should be establishing strong regional organisations, which could later cement continental unity.

Although Tanzania has yet to achieve high levels of economic growth and eradicate poverty, it has nonetheless realised high levels of peace and security, which is more than can be said of numerous countries in sub-Saharan Africa.

Nyerere died in 1999, after having lived a quiet life outside of state office for 14 years.

Kwame Nkrumah, the first president of Ghana (an office he served from March 1957 to February 1966), helped attain his country's independence. In December 1999, he was voted by BBC listeners in Africa as Africa's Man of the Millennium.[6] He was hailed as the *Osagyefo*, which means 'redeemer' in Twi, Ghana's principal language.

Nkrumah was imprisoned by the British in 1950. In 1952 he became the country's first prime minister. After independence in 1957, Ghana became a republic in 1960, with Nkrumah as its first president. Ghana's attainment of independence encouraged other colonies to demand self-rule from the Europeans. Nkrumah became an international symbol of freedom as the leader of the first black African country to become independent of colonial rule. In his first speech, as the clock struck midnight on 5 March 1957 and as the former Gold Coast became Ghana, he declared: 'We are going to see that we create our own African personality and identity. We again rededicate ourselves in the struggle to emancipate other countries in Africa; for our independence is meaningless unless it is linked up with the total liberation of the African continent.'[7]

Nkrumah encouraged industrialisation. He tried to rapidly industrialise Ghana's economy. He argued that for Ghana to become a truly independent state, it had to industrialise in order to escape the colonial trade system by reducing dependence on foreign capital, technology and material goods. Opposed by the Western powers, Nkrumah constructed one of Africa's biggest hydro-electric power plants, the Akosombo Dam on the Volta River in eastern Ghana, which still remains vital to Ghana's industrial development.

Like Nyerere, Nkrumah was also a pan-Africanist and believed in African unity. He explained his African vision in his 1961 book, *I Speak of Freedom*, in which he wrote:

> Divided we are weak; united, Africa could become one of the greatest forces for good in the world. I believe strongly and sincerely that with the deep-rooted wisdom and dignity, the innate respect for human lives, the intense humanity that is our heritage, the African race, united under one federal government, will emerge not as just another world bloc to flaunt its wealth and strength, but as a Great Power whose greatness is indestructible because it is built not on fear, envy and suspicion, nor won at the expense of others, but founded on hope, trust, friendship and directed to the good of all mankind. (Nkrumah, 1961: xii–xiv)[8]

Nkrumah was a founder member of the Organisation of African Unity (OAU), which was established in 1963. In July 2002, South African President Thabo Mbeki, its last chairperson, disbanded it and it was replaced by the African Union (AU).

His ideas were supported by President Sékou Touré of Guinea, another early pan-Africanist, and the first president of Mali, Modibo Keita. Like Nkrumah, Touré viewed African unity as a tool of liberation of the African continent from colonialism and neo-colonialism. These pan-Africanists believed that such liberation could prevent Africa from being divided along racial, ethnic and geographical lines.

How did Nkrumah's tenure end? His undoing is alleged to have been his support for African independence. For example, he gave military support to the anti-British guerrillas in Rhodesia – the present Zimbabwe. The Western powers supported internal conflicts and opposition. They helped bring about the military coup that removed Nkrumah's government from power while he was on a state visit to North Vietnam and China in February 1966. The coup was led by Emmanuel Kwasi Kotoka and the National Liberation Council. According to Stockwell,[9] a former Central Intelligence Agency (CIA) officer, it is claimed that the coup received support from the CIA. President Obote of Uganda suffered the same fate in 1971.[10]

The history of the Congo (later Zaire, now DRC) is one of plunder, coups, assassinations and foreign intrusion. Between 1885 and 1908, after King Leopold of Belgium acquired rights to the Congo, it is estimated that roughly 10 million Congolese died because of foreign exploitation.[11] In June 1960, Patrice Lumumba became prime minister of the Congo, now a republic, having been declared the winner in a general election. Belgium had agreed to hold elections and cede power to the winning party.

On 14 September 1960, just 12 weeks after Lumumba had become prime minister, his government was deposed in a coup led by Joseph Mobutu, with the assistance of the CIA and Belgian troops.[12] Lumumba was subsequently imprisoned and executed by firing squad with the assistance of the Belgian government.[13]

There were powerful economic interests in the Congo, such as minerals, rubber and rivers. Lumumba's leadership was seen as likely to disadvantage the US and Belgium. The neocolonial forces helped Lumumba's overthrow and assassination, and installed Mobutu, who became Congo's puppet actor, serving neocolonial interests for 34 years. Also a pan-Africanist, Lumumba wrote a letter in prison before his death to his wife, Pauline, in which he alluded to his hope for African unity:

> Do not weep for me . . . History will one day have its say; it will
> not be the history taught in the United Nations, Washington, Paris
> or Brussels, but the history taught in the countries that have rid

themselves of colonialism and its puppets. Africa will write its own
history, and both north and south of the Sahara it will be a history
full of glory and dignity.   *(Van Lierde, 1972: 422–423)*

These are the few African leaders whom one can describe as great
statesmen. By contrast, however, several other African leaders
engaged in what one could describe as non-developmental politics.
They chose the path of corruption and nepotism to ensure their
continued stay in power. Many such African leaders were involved
in the plunder of either their countries' natural or financial resources. One such leader was Mobutu Sese Seko of Zaire. Other
postcolonial presidents became brutal dictators, killing their fellow citizens on the basis of rumours and fear that they would be
dethroned. Amin was one of those presidents who killed those they
led because they wanted to stay in power. Nyerere helped remove
Amin from Uganda in 1979. Like Mobutu, Amin died in exile.

Ethnic conflict

In social terms, lack of tolerance and co-existence among different ethnic groups (sometimes referred to as 'tribes'[14]) has had a
negative impact on Africa. This has been worsened by politicians'
political interests. The mayhem that unfolded in Kenya after the
2007 elections, in which more than a thousand people died, was
premised on ethnic rivalry between the Kikuyu and the Luo
peoples. In the 1980s, there was a similar situation in Zimbabwe
when rivalry between the Shona and Ndebele ethnic groups re-
emerged. This caused civil unrest in the northern part of the
country. The 1994 genocide in Rwanda was the result of conflict
between two ethnic groups, the minority Tutsi and majority Hutu.
In Uganda, the Lord's Resistance Army (LRA) rebellion, led by
Joseph Kony, continued for over 20 years because of ethnic factors, among other things.

Postcolonial rule in Nigeria, Rwanda, Uganda, Kenya and several other African states has centred on ethnicity and a failure to adhere to the 'live-and-let-live' dictum. However, these ethnic conflicts have at times been premised on suspicion, with ethnic groups that originate from the current leader's region falsely believing that they are above the law. And certain ethnic groups believe that the other ethnic groups (those to which the leader belongs or is close) are more privileged. Fortunately, some – even those in opposition to the ruling governments in some African countries – are beginning to acknowledge that this is not true.[15] This is a positive development in Africa's struggle to reduce conflict and enter competitive politics. In Uganda, for example, there has been tension between the state and one of the major ethnic groups, the Baganda, which has twice caused political problems. The quest by this large group of people to be given independent status within the republic of Uganda resulted in violence in 1966 and the subsequent death of King Mutesa II in exile in London, in 1969. During every election campaign in Uganda and Kenya, politicians vying for the presidency attempt to garner support from the country's ethnic leaders.

Across the continent, it is common practice for voters to discount merit and base their voting patterns on politicians' ethnicity. Even if a candidate lacks merit, people who belong to his or her ethnic group tend to vote for a politician on the basis of their ethnicity – they view the candidate as their 'son' or 'daughter'.

Within a region and ethnic group, there are also cases of intra-ethnic rivalry between sub-ethnic groups, with sub-groups accusing others of enjoying greater privilege.[16]

Weak civil society

In Africa, most people live in rural areas. There are relatively few large cities. Some countries, such as Uganda, which has a population of over 30 million, have only one main city. But even where there are bigger cities, the rate of urbanisation is still low because of subsistence agriculture and low levels of industrialisation. In 2010, in all the 54 countries of Africa, there were just 52 cities with more than one million people (McKinsey Global Institute, 2010).[17] These cities include those in fairly advanced African countries like Egypt, South Africa and Libya. Citizens in urban centres tend to understand the economic and political situation better than those in rural areas. They have the wherewithal to rise against their oppressors, and they have done so, as testified by the recent events in Arab North Africa.

Many sub-Saharan rural people, on the other hand, know little about life outside their villages. They mainly rely on information from their radios. In some countries, like Zimbabwe, people are forced to listen to propaganda in the media. And because of their limited knowledge, coupled with poor roads, transport links and limited education, they have little contact with other people in the same country facing similar challenges. The effect of this is a lack of a shared national identity.

In Arab North Africa, on the other hand, where most people live in urban areas, have access to TVs and education, a sense of strong civil society has grown. Citizens have been able to organise protests in various towns and cities, and challenged their oppressors and removed them from power.

In communities where there are monarchies or chieftaincies, many people pay more allegiance to such institutions than to the state. This is common in parts of Nigeria and Uganda,[18] and in Swaziland, which is ruled by an absolute monarch, King Mswati.

The combined result of these factors is a weakening of civil society. Many Africans cannot speak with one voice on issues of national concern. However, there is another reason why people in less developed sub-Saharan African countries are constrained in terms of their ability to challenge their leaders over their situation. And that is poverty. In communities where illiteracy and poverty prevail, it is not usual for people to be organised into mass movements and take action against their leaders. How can a person who lives on less than the equivalent of a dollar a day participate in a demonstration for a week? What will the family eat during that week? People live from hand to mouth and do not have savings.

It can be claimed that the people in Arab North Africa (or the Arab Maghreb region) successfully demonstrated against their leaders in 2011, partly because their average per capita income, between $5 000 and $15 000, facilitated their mobilisation, in addition to their exposure to international media and trends of good governance. In 2010 Libya (a nation referred to by the World Bank as being in the upper middle economic bracket) had a per capita income of approximately $17 068; Tunisia's gross domestic product (GDP) per capita was $7 979; Algeria's $8 320; Morocco's $4 628; and Egypt's was above $5 889.[19] The so-called Arab Spring began in Tunisia and the movement spread to Egypt and Libya. Whether the Arab states will embrace Western-style democracy is yet to be seen. They do not have a history of democratic governance of the sort espoused by the West. We discuss the Arab Spring later. We also discuss the effect of foreign intervention under NATO in Libya (and in future in other African countries) for regime change. The point here, however, is that, with the exception of some countries, such as Botswana, Gabon, Mauritius, South Africa and Angola, which enjoy an average per capita income greater than $5 000, the sub-Saharan average GDP per capita in 2010 was around $1 600. A 2010 Gallup survey[20] conducted across the sub-Saharan countries established that a median GDP per capita increased from $1 315 in 2007 to $1 610 in 2010. This is still a very low income. To depend on $1 600 for 12 months means you are living in poverty.

Patriotism and nationalism

Patriotism can be referred to as an ethos whereby citizens are devoted and loyal to their countries. National love and commitment contribute to the success of one's society. Chinua Achebe writes in *The Trouble with Nigeria*:

> A patriot is a person who loves his country. He is not a person who says he loves his country. He is not even a person who shouts and swears or recites and sings his love of his country. He is the one who cares deeply about the happiness and well-being of his country and its people. (Achebe, 1984: 15–16)

According to Leif-Eric Easley (2007) of Harvard University Department of Government, 'nationalism[21] is a sense of loyalty and devotion to a nation, prescribing the promotion of national wealth, power and prestige . . . ' The love for a country is vital to the development of society. Whenever books are written about the factors that have led to the development of China,[22] Malaysia, Singapore, South Korea and others, the authors never clearly discuss the importance of nationalism as a contributing factor. They present only those purely economic factors, such as high rates of growth, and inputs – labour, physical capital and human capital. These countries, however, have achieved higher levels of growth because the people and their leaders are committed to their countries. The leaders explained to the citizens their current poverty levels and the need to commit to development. The citizenry realised that they were poor and needed to work together for growth and development.

It is surprising, therefore, to find that most Africans have little commitment to their countries. This absence of nationalism has bred crime, corruption and political conflict. Most African countries have several ethnic groups brought together by historical factors (as a result of assimilation and colonialism when the boundaries were being drawn). But these are historical legacies that people ought to overcome. Africa has reached a stage when, while reflecting on its historical injustices, it must now start to take control of its own future. Africans need to stay united in their diversity. If ethnic groups continue to behave ethnically (evident, for example, in the negative ethos of those who believe they are Shona or Ndebele before they are Zimbabwean) rather than jointly embracing their national identity, the historical problems will persist. At the national level, the problems will be manifested in ethnic clashes, nepotism and favouritism, regional imbalances and civil wars. Each ethnic group will want a leader who is from their community, and criteria based on merit will die. Bigger ethnic groups are bound to dominate smaller ones, perpetuating the conflicts. Governments, therefore, have a big role to play in inculcating a spirit of nationalism and defusing ethnic tensions. There is a need for media and education campaigns to educate citizens about the benefits of patriotism because the love for one's country is crucial in national development.

Civil wars and internal conflict

Since independence, Africa has experienced wars in the form of internal and cross-border conflicts. In Angola the revolt lasted more than 20 years. In Sudan, the conflict and wars between the predominantly Arab north and the black people of the south lasted over 50 years. According to President Omar al-Bashir[23] of Sudan, the conflicts between the north and south began in 1959. He was quoted as saying: 'The south suffers from many problems. It's been at war since 1959.' This war has sucked in the neighbouring countries of Uganda, Ethiopia and Kenya.

Uganda has had the LRA[24] rebel group conflict for over 24 years. This war is estimated to have cost Uganda more than 400 000 lives. It has also affected the economic activities in the north and part of the West Nile in Uganda. Miguel, Satyanath and Sergenti

(2004) have found that GDP growth is significantly negatively related to the incidence of civil conflict in sub-Saharan Africa. The war in northern Uganda affected the economy in various ways. Given that most rural dwellers in Uganda depend on agriculture, during the war the economy suffers. Agriculture provides food, employment and incomes. Most rural people sell their agricultural surplus production to the market. A Uganda Bureau of Statistics (UBOS) report published in early 2009 shows that while the country's average national poverty rate was 31 per cent, in northern Uganda it was over 60 per cent (UBOS, 2009). The war has led to a generation of youth who have had no formal education. And this was not the first war or internal conflict in Uganda. There were internal wars during Idi Amin and Obote's tenures of office, which also affected production.

Virtually the entire sub-Saharan region has been embroiled in internal conflicts or revolts. Besides Sudan and Uganda, Rwanda, DRC, Nigeria, Madagascar, Angola, Mozambique, Burundi, Somalia, Ethiopia, Eritrea and Zimbabwe have all had periods of political instability, war or internal conflicts. Indeed, only Tanzania, Botswana, Swaziland and Mauritius have had long periods of peace.

Although most African leaders are quick to blame colonialism for the conflicts in their countries, this is not the whole story. The world is never told that selfishness, personal aggrandisement and nepotism have usually led these countries into internal conflicts.

Furthermore, because of the prevalence of several ethnic groups in most African countries (Uganda, Kenya, Zambia, Nigeria and Ghana, to mention but a few), with different local languages and dialects, the potential for civil strife is ever present.

Economists Paul Collier and Anke Hoeffler[25] state that the more a country is ethnically divided, the greater its prospect of civil war. Ethnic divisions explain the higher incidence of civil wars in Africa than in other developing regions, such as southern Asia, in the last 30 years, argues Zambian-born economist Dambisa Moyo. And yet there are several countries with numerous ethnic groups that continue to coexist peacefully. One can mention Tanzania, Kenya (until post-election violence erupted in 2007), Botswana and Zambia. Conversely, there are other countries with very few ethnic groups, which, however, have had civil wars and internal conflicts. Rwanda and Burundi are on the list. In each of these two neighbouring countries there are three main ethnic groups that even speak the same language (Tutsi, Hutu and Twa), but these countries have experienced violent conflict.

In Nigeria, there have been conflicts over oil. The people in the oil-producing region, the Niger Delta, would like to enjoy a meaningful share of the revenue from the oil. But it is no secret that leaders in Nigeria have been involved in corruption. The region has experienced high levels of youth unemployment (and these youths have turned into 'terrorists' in the region), perceived discrimination against employment of the locals by the mining companies, pollution due to the fumes from oil and gas extraction, and neglect by successive regimes of federal Nigeria's central government. There is also the perception among the minority ethnic groups in the Niger Delta that the non-oil-producing majority who control the federal government are in partnership with multinational oil companies (Cyril, 2009).

In *The Costs of Violence* (Miller et al., 2009), the World Bank puts the case that the costs of internal conflict include the loss of life (at least 16 million people); destruction of crops, buildings and infrastructure; the cost of arms; the wages or opportunity cost of soldiers or guerrillas; the cost of injuries and psychological incapacitation (which can be long-lasting); and long-term consequences on investment and economic growth.[26]

In budgetary terms, the cost of war has been estimated or quantitatively analysed by academics.[27] In their article *The Challenge of Reducing the Global Incidence of Civil War*, Paul Collier and Anke

Hoeffler have put the cost of a seven-year conflict at $64 billion (Collier & Hoeffler, 2004). As we have seen, some wars or conflicts in Africa last more than 25 years so these figures may have to be multiplied. If the causes of civil war and internal conflicts in Africa are clear to the leaders, why are solutions hard to come by? Greed, personal interests and lack of commitment to national aspirations may explain this to a certain extent. I take the view that the sharing of power after a flawed election is a case of pure selfishness and greed.

Disease and the silent leadership

Most writers have identified disease as one of those causes of sub-Saharan Africa's economic decline. In conditions of poverty, absence of a clean environment and malnutrition, diseases exacerbate the cycle of suffering. Before the polio vaccine, this disease killed many people in Africa and those who narrowly survived it remained maimed. Today malaria and HIV/AIDS are major health scourges. Although the authorities were aware of HIV/AIDS[28] by around 1985, the African leaders of the day kept silent about it. In the late 1980s, only the Ugandan administration began a crusade against HIV/AIDS, which involved civil society and religious organisations. Meanwhile, in neighbouring Kenya, the leaders kept quiet about HIV/AIDS. Although there is no documented covert or overt government policy to this effect, it is claimed that Kenya did not want to deter tourists. President Thabo Mbeki of South Africa implied that AIDS was a cultural syndrome; he also linked AIDS to poverty. He refused to accept the scientifically[29] proven facts that HIV is the sole cause of AIDS. Mbeki's belief is that a virus cannot cause a syndrome because a syndrome is a group of diseases resulting from acquired immune deficiency.[30]

In Swaziland, instead of encouraging his people to understand the AIDS pandemic, King Mswati continued to annually attend the traditional reed dance in order to choose young wives. In Swaziland, the prevalence of HIV/AIDS was at around 40 per cent before 2003. According to the report by the Joint UN Programme on HIV/AIDS (UNAIDS), *Aids Epidemic Update: 2009*, approximately 190 000 people in Swaziland are HIV-positive, including 15 000 children under the age of 15 (UNAIDS, 2009). And the average Swazi life expectancy fell by half between 1990 and 2007, in great part due to the epidemic.[31]

The socio-economic effects of HIV/AIDS are innumerable. The pandemic has claimed the lives of breadwinners, leaving vulnerable children at the mercy of their environment. And the syndrome continues to affect children. It has affected the budgetary allocations of all sub-Saharan African countries. Every year HIV/AIDS has to be taken into account in national budgets and funds have to be put aside for the fight against it. The health budget has subsequently risen dramatically in most sub-Saharan countries, increasing their demand for development assistance. In some countries, the HIV/AIDS package has been allocated and utilised optimally; in others, it was seen as manna from heaven by greedy politicians.

In brief, silence on the part of administrations and subsequent misuse of donor money have exacerbated the HIV/AIDS crisis in much of Africa.

Culture and economic growth

Culture is very important in shaping the growth of an economy, as it influences savings and consumer behaviour. Renowned economist and development expert, Amartya Sen, in his article *How Does Culture Matter?* (Sen, 2004) presents seven ways in which culture influences development: culture as a constitutive part of development; economically remunerative cultural activities and objects; cultural factors influencing economic behaviour;[32] culture and political participation, social solidarity and association;

cultural sites and recollection of past heritage; and cultural influences on value formation and evolution.

As a cultural reference group, the family influences one's choice of whom to marry, the number of children one will have, the investment decisions we make and our consumption habits. In most developing countries, the family is a very important entity in terms of wealth creation and ownership. For example, in rural sub-Saharan communities, the choice of whom to marry is a very important one because the extended family means that fewer family members work, but more eat. Even political decisions on who to vote for are agreed on as a family. Such is the traditional (cultural) way of living in Africa in the age of globalisation.

Culture and religion have been hotbeds of ethnic tension and conflict in sub-Saharan Africa. The solution to achieving harmony between different cultures is for political and civic leaders with foresight to cultivate a spirit of harmonious co-existence. Political appointments should also reflect cultural diversity.

Savings culture

Savings behaviour is very important because of the close relationship between savings[33] and economic growth. Developed, developing and less developed economies have varying levels of income and wealth. In developed countries, income tends to be evenly distributed, whereas in poor countries income tends to be distributed unevenly. The savings culture in Africa has been a concern for development strategies. In economic terms, when a person saves, it means he/she has forgone consumption and, therefore, has money for investment. The more a person saves, the less he/she spends on consumption. This is referred to as postponed consumption, and taking into consideration the time value of money, the person who saves is expected to live better in the future. While trying to explain the causes of the different levels of development in Africa and Asia, by comparing South Korea and Ghana, Huntington (1991), while acknowledging that several other factors are responsible, says that savings culture played a large part. The reasons why the South Koreans were more developed than Ghanaians included the culture of valuing savings and investment, hard work, discipline and education. Ghana, on the other hand, lacked these values.[34] Huntington believes, therefore, that culture played a big role in suppressing Ghana's economic growth, while South Korea became an industrial and advanced country. While giving a keynote address (*Cultures in the 21st century: Conflicts and convergences*) on 4 February 1999 at Colorado College's 125th anniversary symposium, Huntington said that 'South Koreans valued thrift, savings, and investment, hard work, discipline, and education. Ghanaians had different values.' (Huntington, 1999)

A higher propensity to save results in a lower propensity to consume. For most Asian countries, savings form about 20 per cent of one's income. In Japan it is about 18 per cent; and less than 5 per cent in Africa. According to Bloomberg's *Business Week*,[35] China has one of the highest savings rates in the world, at 38 per cent, and India at 34.7 per cent. Therefore, during the process of economic growth and poverty reduction, individuals require a culture of saving and investment, as shown by China, India and Japan. Based on the average savings rate in Africa, it is obvious that a poor savings culture has negatively affected the economic performance of some African countries. They have, therefore, been left behind other developing countries in Asia and Latin America.

Africa should therefore adopt a culture of saving for the future. Investment is facilitated by savings. A starting point is for government to initiate an aggressive campaign to encourage locals to save and invest.

Dictatorship or leadership?

African politics has become a zero-sum game in which the winner-takes-all leadership philosophy prevails. Democratic institutions give way to a concentration of power in the presidency. There have emerged what we can refer to as weak states led by powerful dictators who are above the law, as opposed to benevolent leaders. Dictators make their citizens dependants of the state and not participants in the country's economic and political development. Dictators are patrons waiting to be showered with praises, and there are many to be found in the sub-Saharan region. They are not simply strongmen but tyrants. Africa has had notorious examples of such leaders: Amin and his friend Mobutu, and, recently, Robert Mugabe, for example. This book concentrates on strong leaders, whether men or women.

Benevolent leaders are charismatic, and history has shown that they have brought success to their people and societies. We can define benevolent leadership as the process of creating a virtuous cycle of encouraging, initiating and implementing positive change in organisations through, among others, inspiring hope and fostering courage for positive action, and ultimately leaving a legacy and positive impact for the larger community.

Benevolent leaders act as agents of positive change in organisations. They are not strongmen or women (i.e. dictators), but they are strong leaders[36] who guide their communities to a bright future, who emphasise domestic growth and embrace democracy. Strong leaders are focused on setting objectives and work with their teams to achieve them.

Such leaders can be found anywhere in the world, including Africa. They include Ghandi of India, Martin Luther King of the US, Mandela of South Africa, Lee Kwan Yu of Singapore and Park Chung-Hee of South Korea. Such leaders are often not viewed as democratic, in the Western sense of the term, but more as visionaries. They start to build their societies' road to success. The West referred to Lee Kwan Yew and Park Chung-Hee as dictators and to Mandela as a communist. But even when no longer in office, the majority of their people (and even renowned Western political science scholars) still hold such leaders in high esteem,[37] a clear indication of their leadership skills and ability to advance society. Huntington suggests that Lee Kwan Yew, who led Singapore for decades, gave that country political leadership and was determined to create a non-corrupt society, which in large part he did (Huntington, 1999).

Instead of leaders who have been committed to helping eradicate poverty, ignorance and disease from society, unfortunately Africa has had liars, thieves and tyrannical dictators. In post-independence Africa, there have been a number of leaders who believed that they were more important than the states they led. And in economic terms, they may have been correct. They directly or indirectly owned most of their countries' resources. There are still a number of such leaders today. They are the government and the private sector. If an investor meets the government, they meet them, and when they want to meet the private sector for partnerships, they meet the same person. Such leaders have no interest in concepts such as patriotism or nationalism. For any project to succeed, they ask, 'What is in it for me?'

In most of the poorly led African countries, decisions that affect national development are usually made by informal networks of influential persons who are close to power. Never mind that some of these persons may also have formal positions in government. In such countries, public jobs are subject to tests of loyalty to the 'big man' rather than the merit of the applicant. The argument here is that one cannot give a powerful position to a person who is not on your political side.[38] The applicant has to be vetted or screened. There is no problem with screening per se[39] – they do it in Canada, the UK and the US. The problem is

that the vetting or screening is used as a way of denying opportunities to those who do not belong to the regime in power. Jobs
or scholarships are not given on merit, but on whether the applicant supports those in power. Poor leadership has created dissent
and breeds political unrest. So leadership is a key issue in determining whether a country succeeds or fails.

Committed leadership or
multi-party democracy?

'Democracy and open markets will only be accepted for
what they deliver, not for what they promise.'
(Benjamin William Mkapa, former president of Tanzania)[1]

Africa and Asia were both once colonised by Europeans. However, the difference in growth levels between these two continents, as mentioned earlier, is startling. While African leaders continue to blame history (i.e. colonialism) there is hypocrisy in the failure to point the finger at the factors that originate within Africa, which are among the main causes of poverty and economic failure on the beautiful continent.

When the colonialists left Asia, the Asians undertook to establish their nations as key competitors and players in the global stage. The story of Lee Kwan-Yew and his mark on Singapore[2] is well known. Indeed, he has told the story himself in *From Third World to First World: The Singapore Story 1965–2000.* Singapore is not the only state that managed to achieve impressive growth in the Asian region because of strong, visionary leaders. The Republic of South Korea is another example. Park Chung-Hee (see page 41-42) is considered by many in South Korea as the father of the so-called Miracle of the Han River, namely the economic success story of South Korea. He can be regarded as a leader who had a vision for that country. He is remembered as the one who started the process of Korea's economic take-off. South Korea currently exports vehicles (e.g. Hyundai, Kia), electronics, fridges and other manufactured goods.

We cannot say that the Asian boom nations have ample natural resources. Neither do they benefit from high levels of Western-style democratisation.[3] China has achieved high levels of growth and realised more exports globally without Western-style democracy. It portrays itself as a communist state with a market-oriented policy, and it is still regarded as a developing country by the UN, US and Europe. According to the World Trade Organisation (WTO), in 2009 China overtook Germany to become the world's leading exporter.[4] According to the US–China Business Council in Washington, China is the US's third largest export market globally.[5]

Relationship between democracy and growth

Some scholars have begun to question what comes first when looking at the relationship between democracy and growth. This discussion is relevant to Africa – and indeed all the developing world.

While agreeing that economic freedom promotes growth, some scholars doubt whether more political freedom improves economic performance.[6] The argument that what is important is not democracy but having in place the rule of law and policies that improve economic freedom (without necessarily having fully developed political institutions) is exemplified by Augusto Pinochet's regime in Chile. Under Pinochet, Chile achieved a high level of growth without a fully developed democracy, and not all institutions were in place. There were key organisations in place to promote competitiveness.

According to Robert Barro in his article Democracy and Growth, the favourable effects on growth include maintenance of the rule of law, free markets, small government consumption and high human capital (Barro, 1996). He adds that once these variables and the initial level of per capita growth are held constant, the overall effect of democracy on growth is weakly negative. This means that once a government (democratic or otherwise) has put in place conditions that improve economic freedom, then growth can be achieved in either a democratic political system or an authoritarian one.

As an aspect of democracy, periodic elections do not result in tangible political change in most African states. Why is this the case? In most developing African countries, elections are rigged. It is also alleged to have happened in Florida during George W. Bush's elections in 2000[7] and 2004.[8] In Africa there is ballot buying. During elections in Africa, some leaders will win by a very large margin because of election malpractices. Some experts in Africa have begun questioning the rationale of having regular elections,[9] and even doubt whether voters are capable of deciding on the future of their countries.[10]

Countries that have not yet achieved higher levels of growth require committed and visionary leadership that can steer the state and put forward sound micro- and macro-level policies that will attract investment, boost production and increase exports. I have already mentioned such leaders as Nelson Mandela, Kwame Nkrumah and Julius Nyerere. It would be difficult to add more names to this list. This is because some leaders come to power promising to deliver their people to the 'biblical promised land of Canaan' but later leave no trace of history worth recording.

Dambisa Moyo, in her book *Dead Aid*, puts it thus: 'Far from being a prerequisite for economic growth, democracy can hamper development as democratic regimes find it difficult to push economically beneficial legislation amid rival parties and jockeying interests.' (Moyo, 2009: 42)[11] If Rwanda or Uganda succeeds economically, it will not necessarily be because of regular elections, but rather the commitment of their leadership to promoting sound macroeconomic policies that enhance economic growth; and also winning the war against corruption in public offices.

When one considers the nations of Arab Africa and the phenomenon of the so-called Arab Spring, it is evident that when these countries were experiencing lower levels of growth and development, there were no demonstrations against leaders over-staying in office. It is after they attained sound levels of growth and higher levels of per capita income ranging from $5000 for Egypt to around $15000 for Libya that people began to demonstrate and force the leaders out of power. The sub-Saharan countries' per capita are lower. For example, the central Africa's average per capita is $466, West Africa is $441 and East Africa $303.[12] In other words, people in Arab Africa can literally afford to demonstrate for weeks; they have sufficient money to pay for essentials such as food and housing.

During their growth and development, most of the powerful Asian states were not democratic. China is viewed as undem-ocratic by the West, yet, as already pointed out above, it has achieved very rapid economic growth. It could, therefore, be ar-gued that in sub-Saharan Africa, economic growth should precede democracy. The author does not advocate following this path to economic growth – it is purely an observation based on the exam-ple of the Asian countries.

Patriotism and visionary leadership

It has been observed by scholars and practitioners that good leadership is a key to success. It is important at the corporate and national levels. Good leadership comes with commitment. Bad leaders have undermined the progress of some African states. Some writers, however, have tended to associate this solely with a lack of democracy. And others have pointed to these leaders' appetite for rent-seeking activities. Lack of democracy does have an effect on society. However, one cannot ignore these leaders' lack of vision and commitment to their societies as important factors. Leaders who are not committed to development often tend to be corrupt and, therefore, engage in rent-seeking activities.

Countries that have committed leaders[13] have witnessed strong and positive GDP growth. Committed heads of state and government understand that their countries have a development problem and that they can provide the type of leadership to resolve this. Some have fought serious battles to oust wrong leaders. Some have sacrificed their families' happiness in a bid to serve their brethren. They work with advisory teams and design relevant policies and legislation. Such leaders take the time to groom teams of future leaders and specialists; they appoint the right types of experts. They also make an effort to understand how the private sector operates. With such leadership, growth does not happen by chance (the *deus ex machina*) – it is planned, implemented and monitored.

The problem facing Africa is not primarily long spells of dictatorship but leaders who are unpatriotic and uncommitted to their countries. Many are mercenaries looking for something to plunder. The experience of Singapore, South Korea and China shows that developing countries require economic growth, industrialisation and eventually fully fledged democratic institutions – in that order. What currently matters most in Africa is that the leaders should push strongly the economic development agenda and create an enabling environment for private-sector competitiveness to thrive. Eventually, development and democracy should then bed in.

The 'I am an American' spirit is strong among citizens of the US. An American is a citizen of the US first and foremost. This spirit is reinforced in the US by the encouragement of voluntary military service for the youth before they choose their career path. Such military service is vital for instilling a spirit of nationalism.

The US also benefits from a system whereby the president serves only two terms of office, however good he or she may be. Therefore, past leaders, such as Bill Clinton and George Bush, who served two terms each, will never get another chance at the White

House. This kind of arrangement was established based on conditions particular to the US, but countries in the other parts of the world, including Africa, have copied it.

On the other hand, the UK and Canada have open-ended terms of office. Leaders chosen by their party can remain in power for as long as their parties elect them and as long as they win national elections. Had Jean Chrétien, Prime Minister of Canada, 1993–2003, not lost popularity within the party and had the party not thought he would be an unpopular national leader, he would have stood again. The Canadian constitution would have permitted him to continue in office for another five-year term. Former British prime minister Margaret Thatcher was in power for 11 years. And she could have gone on if her party had still wanted her: the UK system imposes no limits to a leader's tenure in office, other than the requirement for general elections. The political ethos in the UK and Canada is that if a leader still has something good to offer, then why limit them? Like the US, the UK and Canada have realised long-term economic growth and achieved development under their systems. The UK, Canada and the US have prospered under their different political arrangements; all three are developed nations. The question is, which of the two systems should African countries adopt in order to realise sustained economic growth and development?

There are leaders who have stayed long in power in Asia, the Middle East and Africa, but who have ensured that their countries realise sustained economic growth. There are also those who have seen their countries go down the drain.

Consider Botswana in sub-Saharan Africa. Since its independence in 1966, Botswana has been governed by one party, the Botswana Democratic Party (BDP). Botswana is Africa's longest-running multi-party democracy, and is also regarded as Africa's least corrupt nation. Its population is among Africa's wealthiest. The country's president is also the president of the long-ruling

BDP, and there are concerns that both constitutional and political power are highly centralised in the presidency. Furthermore, the president is not directly elected by the people. This brings us to the crux of the issue: democracy will follow growth. The Botswanan example shows that economic empowerment, reduced poverty and development can be achieved in that order. Then democratisation will emerge. And at this level, democratic pressure cannot be stopped.

Let us take the example of Uganda. After a five-year bush war, former National Resistance Army rebels took over power in Uganda in 1986. They introduced a system of government that worked right from the village up to the national parliament, based on individual merit. Individuals, and not the political party, presented their manifestos to the electorate. The electorate, in turn, chose the right representative based on their credentials and other factors. Some observers, historians and development writers have argued that it was during this period that Uganda had one of the most vibrant parliaments in sub-Saharan Africa.

Meanwhile, Uganda's development partners continued to oppose this system of governance (maybe because it was not like that of the US or UK, or other developed states), and in 2001 Uganda reverted to a multi-party dispensation. Now there are allegations that Uganda has a parliament polarised into different parties. There are claims that when an issue is not good for the nation, party members are compelled to support it without question. In situations where more than 65 per cent of the legislators are members of one party, and there is a party chief whip making sure that party members toe the party line, what can the opposition achieve? It is unlikely that the minority will benefit from such a system. This is an example of Western-style competitive politics, which Uganda has had to embrace. The system may have worked well in the West, but it is not beneficial in poor African countries where the voter is ignorant of the candidates' political credentials. Voters are not agenda- or issue-driven when voting, and they may not even know why they are voting. Evidence has shown that they can be induced to cast their ballots.

Ugandan President Yoweri Museveni, during his stay in power, has made his country stand out in terms of its economic growth, especially private-sector-led growth, and in the fight against HIV/AIDS. When Museveni came to power in 1986, Uganda's GDP was 3.4 trillion Ugandan shillings. In 2010 it rose to 37.5 trillion Ugandan shillings (equivalent to $17 billion) and in 2011 it was 39 trillion Ugandan shillings, a twelve-fold increase in the size of the economy. In his 16 years in office, the Rwandan president, Paul Kagame, has transformed the small nation's misfortunes into fortune and growth. We can conclude that those African countries that are doing well economically have a committed leadership, irrespective of their leaders' duration in office.

In Africa, where most leaders have betrayed their people's hopes, most opposition politicians and several academics blame the problems on leaders overstaying in power (and they are not completely wrong, as, indeed, some leaders have had long spells in office and with negative results, going by all the indicators of progress). This is not, however, to mean that staying in power for long is necessarily a negative factor. The problems occur when those who remain in power fail to implement a successful agenda for development.

Arab Spring, regime change and violent foreign intervention in Africa

The time comes when a leader, whether they have served their people well or not, has to vacate the seat. Nature may take its course: they grow old or die. There is also the issue of inertia and citizens just getting fed up with their leaders. In Arab North Africa, the latter was evident in 2011 in the regime-change protests in

Tunisia, Egypt and Libya – countries where people rose up against their leaders. In Libya's case there is a growing debate in Africa, and to some extent in the West, about who actually removed Gaddafi from power. Some claim that it was the North Atlantic Treaty Organisation (NATO) and not the Libyan people themselves. Others believe that a combination of oil and mining interests, tribal conflicts and the West's hatred for Gaddafi led to his being ousted.

What is important is not the removal of a leader, but the future of a state in terms of growth and development. The Arab Spring has been and gone, but will it deliver peace, stability and development in the region? Will it diminish internal conflicts due to ethnicity and Islamism, and bring about a more even share of national wealth? Will it enhance democracy? Will it reduce the trend of young people in the region being conscripted into terrorist organisations? Is the removal of a leader enough for a state to achieve these goals?

It is difficult to predict the outcome of these ongoing processes of change. Given the composition and nature of the region, several scenarios are likely. The assumption and hope is that the region will head towards a greater degree of democracy; that new leaders will emerge and respect the rule of law; that they will observe human rights and not discriminate against or tyrannise their people; that women will be given equal rights, etc. But there is a genuine fear that the region could be headed towards a different type of autocracy,[14] where fundamental Islamist organisations replace the old leaders with new autocratic leaders. Some observers have suggested that this will eventually happen in Egypt.

The world will have to wait patiently to see to what degree the Islamist parties in Tunisia and the Muslim brotherhood in Egypt manage the dimensions of democracy. The Islamist parties have taken over in Tunisia and Egypt. They are in control in Tunisia and they have won the majority in parliament in Egypt. They were supported by the Gulf states for the purposes of Islamising

Egypt. They are likely to stifle religious and social freedoms and impose strict religious rules. These countries are most likely to create fused political and religious states in which religious instructions, laws, codes and ways of life are upheld by the state. Democracy and human freedoms may be limited.

During the period of the Arab Spring (or Arab Awakening), three leaders were toppled from power and one assassinated: Ben Ali of Tunisia, Egypt's Hosni Mubarak and Muammar Gaddafi of Libya. This had never happened in this region before. It was a surprise to the leaders who were removed and it was a surprise to the leaders in other African countries. And it was indeed a surprise to the leaders in the Western world, who at first failed to applaud those on the winning side because they were still unsure whether it was becoming a reality. At first, the US supported Mubarak until the winds of change turned into a hurricane. What are the factors that favoured the Arab Spring, and what are its implications for other leaders and dictators in Africa?

Firstly, many people in the region live in urban centres so it was easy to mobilise them. The elite in urban centres are usually the mobilisers for a revolution. They understand the lifestyle of their leaders, who also live in cities, and they follow events in the press. It is much more difficult to mobilise peasants in villages for political change. The per capita income in Arab Africa is higher than in sub-Saharan Africa: the Arabs were literally able to afford to demonstrate. In Uganda, for instance, the opposition started what they called the walk-to-work demonstrations in 2011, but they did not plan them for all the week. They understood that people would eventually have to abandon the protest and look at providing food for the family. During the Arab North African revolutions, the Arabic language was a unifying factor. In other parts of Africa, language is likely to be a barrier. Religion is also a potent mobilising factor in the Arab world – Islam was key to the success of the Arab Spring.

The implications of this surprising series of revolutions are likely to be manifold. Firstly, the new leaders will promise 'window dressing' changes to their people. Secondly, they will strengthen their state apparatus to quickly crack down on dissenters. This is counter-productive. Thirdly, they will negotiate deals with the opposition, so that the opposition will reduce the speed of mobilisation. Fourth, they will be quick to sign deals with Western leaders. This will give them time to think about their future.

To the citizens of other African countries, the Arab Spring gives hope to those who feel that it could happen in their countries. As we have seen, however, the sociopolitical architecture in sub-Saharan Africa is different from Arab North Africa, though these states may be faced with similar challenges: poor governance, corruption, poverty and human rights issues. But the people are scared, and more scared about what happened in Libya than elsewhere. They are scared of regime change supported by NATO and the US, or any form of regime change from 'above'.

After the September 11 attacks, President Bush hinted at the need for regime change in other countries. He proposed the war on terror as a way of eliminating regimes that his administration considered were likely to support terrorism or were considered dictatorships by the then US leadership. His strategy was applied to Saddam Hussein of Iraq, who was removed from power and later executed.

After Bush's two terms expired and he left the White House, next came President Obama. Though he may not have put it as such to the media, it seems he also espoused the regime-change strategy and approved of the Bush administration's foreign military strategy. Obama appointed Bush's defence secretary, Mr Robert Gates, as his new defence secretary. Obama also promised to work with Africans to realise democracy and good governance. While visiting Ghana, Obama addressed the parliament[15] and told them that the time for dictators was over. It is, therefore, safe to say that US foreign policy a decade ago and today is one and the same.

Gaddafi and NATO forces

When Obama won the presidential race, Gaddafi said he feared that he would suffer from an inferiority complex because he was not white. Ironically, Gaddafi died an ignominious death at the hands of Obama's military. Although the boots of American soldiers did not literally set foot on Libyan soil, unmanned US planes performed the military task of flushing out the Libyan army and ended Gaddafi's regime.

The US was not alone in taking out Gaddafi, however. It worked with NATO, and mainly France and the UK. They supported mainly those groups that are ethnically opposed to the Gaddafi regime – and now Libya has new people in government. There are still skirmishes between these ethnic groups and it is not yet safe to declare this country as being in a better situation than before. It will take time before there is harmony, peace and stability. It will also take some time before Libya becomes a truly democratic country – from the viewpoint of the West. It is true that Gaddafi's opponents were many and that he treated others badly. He had little respect for certain fellow leaders in Africa and other parts of the world. He was too powerful to have been able to be removed by the weak Libyan opposition alone. The EU and US under NATO came in and helped put an end to his regime. Good governance is pivotal for development, and ultimately democracy is important for each society. But, as Obama said in Ghana, 'each nation gives life to democracy in its own way, and in line with its own traditions . . . The essential truth of democracy is that each nation determines its own destiny.'[16] This statement is vitally important. Democracy should not be imported or imposed by foreigners or their institutions from above. It should be demanded and fought for by the citizens themselves. This is when democracy will last.

There is a contention in Africa, one that is supported by former President Mbeki[17] of South Africa and scholars, that it was not the power of the people but foreign intervention that ended Gaddaffi's rule in Libya. It was only in Tunisia and Egypt, they argue, that the people rose against and removed their leaders – and without a gun. In Libya it was not people demonstrating and calling their leaders to leave office, but citizens with foreign support who took up arms and fought the leadership.

What happened in Libya can be likened to what happened in Ivory Coast, where a French-sponsored coup led to the overthrow of President Laurent Gbagbo in April 2011. A NATO-led offensive in Libya toppled Colonel Gaddafi a few months later. This was despite African Union intercessions for internal solutions to the political crises in both countries. Indeed, it can be said that when Obama stated that 'the West has often approached Africa as a patron or a source of resources rather than a partner'[18], he was on the mark.

The private sector and managing resources

Once the colonialists had left, in most cases having established infrastructure and sound healthcare facilities, many African leaders took over the mantle of leadership and started enjoying themselves. However, many of them failed to understand the role of the private sector in boosting economic growth, and hence ended up destroying their economies. Zaire (DRC), a country rich in natural resources (diamonds, gold, coltan, etc.) became a habitual beggar for donor aid under Mobutu, and it has not still emerged from that unfortunate position.

In 1972, Idi Amin of Uganda expelled an estimated 80 000 Asians, mainly Indians of British citizenship who owned businesses in Uganda, in what he dubbed 'an economic war'. More than four decades later, the scars of his action remain. A similar situation took place in Zimbabwe. President Mugabe, in the twilight of his political career,[1] decided to give land to those who do not know how to manage business, in an attempt to please those who had been affected by colonial land ownership. And Mugabe has started to nationalise private companies. Irrespective of the political history and other social issues in this country, his narrow understanding of the role of private investments ruined Zimbabwe's economy. He destroyed one of Africa's best performing economies.

Among other reasons, it has been argued that such leaders do not understand that wealth is created at firm or farm level by individual businesses or households, and that it is the private sector that does business and government's role is purely to provide legislation and the necessary facilitative environment. The role of government is to provide an enabling environment to support the private sector, thereby enhancing growth; government needs to influence, facilitate and regulate the private sector.

Failure to understand the state's role in enhancing economic growth in a private sector-led economy has continued to breed conflicts between government and the private sector. There is confusion over the roles that governments should play. Governments should not ignore their vital duties of regulation; neither should they forget to influence what happens in the economy. Governments should only intervene, however, when there is market failure, where there are distortions in the market economy. Governments also need to allocate resources to the social sector via the national budget. The free-market system operates well where government has provided the infrastructure necessary for business – roads, railways, ports and harbours, and public information – and the public institutions to promote private-sector competitiveness: the judiciary, police, investment and export agencies, fiscal institutions, among others.

Sound economic management

Economic management has to be undertaken as a planned, deliberate process by government. The economy cannot grow without a strategic plan focusing on the core competencies and available resources of a country. There is a need for an enabling environment for businesses to engage in the production, marketing and sale of their products. Government must put in place systems, policies, plans and laws to enhance economic growth and development. The plans have objectives, namely what is intended to be achieved. The period in which the planned objectives are to be achieved should also be clearly set out. These plans are a guiding framework for the government and should include expenditure, key sectors to boost and investors to attract. Once these plans, policies, laws and institutions are in place, then all players ought to be made aware of their existence. The stage is now set for all stakeholders to play their part. The practice in sub-Saharan Africa is not that countries do not have good laws and policies, but that the populace are not aware of them – laws and acts tend to be 'hidden' inside government offices.

At the macro-level, the policies and laws needed to facilitate a conducive business and investment environment include good banking laws, investment codes, anti-trust laws, ownership and property rights, especially for businesses, and fair and predictable taxes.

Nations also require policies and plans for enhancing growth within key sectors, such as agriculture, mining, industry, tourism, transport, infrastructure and education, among others. Such policies and plans need to be well thought out and well presented if they are to guide the country in its budgeting for pro-growth strategies, and are necessary in order to realise and sustain high levels of GDP growth.

Plans and policies on reproductive health, family planning, disease control and nutrition will ensure that a country has a healthy population able to contribute physically and mentally to national development. It has been alleged that during the implementation of economic liberalisation, external pressure has often forced sub-Saharan governments to go against national planning. If this has happened, then it was unfortunate and those who accepted this advice betrayed their citizens.

Africa and liberal economic development policies

The Washington consensus and Africa's development failure
A development framework that had been suggested for Latin

America was superimposed on Africa and the results are not rosy. If we look critically at the Washington consensus,[2] we will discover that, according to Nobel laureate and former chief economist at the World Bank, Joseph Stiglitz, in his book *Globalization and its Discontents*, fiscal austerity, privatisation and market liberalisation[3] were the three pillars of Washington consensus advice advocated through the 1980s and 1990s. Stiglitz put it that the Washington consensus policies were designed to respond to the very real problems in Latin America, and that they made considerable sense there. In that part of the world, governments during the 1980s had got their countries into problems, such as running huge deficits, operating inefficient public enterprises and loose monetary policies. It, therefore, made sense to adopt the three pillars of the Washington consensus. Governments in this region needed to divest the role of running enterprises, which could be done better by the private sector. The government would then concentrate on essential public-service provision. The problem, however, was that a remedy that had been suggested for one region, Latin America, based on its particular conditions and problems, was applied as a global solution (and at times viewed as a panacea) for all less-developed countries' problems.

The International Monetary Fund (IMF), for example, strongly pursued privatisation and liberalisation at a faster pace, and, according to Stiglitz, this often imposed very real costs on countries. However, before a policy can be implemented, it is imperative that concerned officials understand the implications in detail. Most governments embraced these policies and quickly began to implement them. To implement a new policy or strategy requires that you consider a gradual approach. Quickly stopping one strategy or policy and then implementing a new one may cause scarcity and also affect certain sections of the society. Before a policy is implemented, those that are likely to be impacted by it need to be informed. Imagine a situation whereby government formerly supplied products to farmers, and then with market liberalisation this stopped. The effect would be that those businesses would collapse, and society would fail to have the services they were previously enjoying.

Public enterprises were sold before there were suitable regulations in place for a competitive environment. In some cases, these enterprises were sold to quack investors. In Uganda, the publicly owned Uganda Commercial Bank was first sold to a quack firm, allegedly based in Malaysia, before it was later resold to Stanbic Bank of South Africa. In Ivory Coast, the public telephone company was privatised before the country had established a regulatory framework to address competitiveness issues (Stiglitz, 2002). The effect was that the French buyers, who had convinced the government and were given a monopoly status of the telephone business, charged extremely high prices. This meant that Internet services were too expensive for ordinary people and students.

Elements of the Washington consensus

Washington consensus	• Fiscal discipline
	• Redirection of public expenditure priorities toward fields offering both high economic returns and the potential to improve income distribution, such as primary healthcare, primary education and infrastructure
	• Tax reform (to lower marginal rates and broaden the tax base)
	• Interest rate liberalisation
	• A competitive exchange rate
	• Trade liberalisation
	• Liberalisation of inflows of foreign direct investment
	• Privatisation
	• Deregulation (to abolish barriers to entry and exit)
	• Secure property rights

Augmented Washington consensus	• Corporate governance
	• Anti-corruption
	• Flexible labour markets
	• WTO agreements
	• Financial codes and standards
	• 'Prudent' capital-account opening
	• Non-intermediate exchange rate regimes
	• Independent central banks/inflation targeting
	• Social safety nets
	• Targeted poverty reduction

Sources: http://www.cid.harvard.edu/cidtrade/issues/washingtonlink.html#_2; (accessed on 26 October 2010) and Rodrik, D., 2001. *The Global Governance of Trade as if Development Really Mattered.* New York: UNDP

Step-by-step economic liberalisation

There is still much debate on whether economically less-developed countries should liberalise trade. The World Bank, learning from the 1990s, has accepted that trade liberalisation is not a panacea for economic development.

However, the World Bank also argues that evidence in some countries shows that economies that have liberalised have registered rapid growth. China, on the other hand, has developed in the last 25 years under strictly government-guided market strategies.

Although, as Stiglitz suggests, there are benefits to be had by opening up the economy, if these measures are pushed through hastily in poor economies it can create serious challenges, such as unemployment, hunger and even death. Sector-by-sector liberalisation can bring in good results in the long term.

There are still concerns surrounding the privatisation of key national enterprises, such as telecommunications and water utility companies.

Natural resources: A blessing or a curse?

Most African nations should be wealthy because of their abundant mineral resources (oil, diamonds, gold, coltan, etc.), but they have remained beggar states and many are dependent on foreign aid. These countries have experienced resource management policy failures and, in turn, have become embroiled in political conflict. Many of the continent's countries that have failed or are lagging behind in their efforts to realise development or reduce absolute poverty are rich in mineral deposits and other natural resources. The Central African Republic is rich in diamonds; Nigeria is rich in oil; the DRC has diamonds, gold, coltan, uranium, oil and gas. It also has natural forests and rivers. Congo Brazzaville is rich in diamonds, as is Sierra Leone; Uganda has gold, oil and uranium; Tanzania has tanzanite and diamonds, as well as the natural resources of harbours and beaches.

But despite all this natural wealth, these countries are still losers in the economic sphere. Although these minerals have made other countries wealthy (even when they buy these minerals from Africa), the absolute poverty levels in these resource-rich African countries are among the highest in the world. Why is it that most of these countries are aid recipients, yet, ideally, they should be donors? The answer to this paradox lies in the fact that the leaders in most of these countries have used the revenue from these resources to enrich themselves. Often the mining or extraction contracts are in the hands of the relatives of the people in power. And when foreign investors are used, they are just decoys. These leaders enjoy private profit and the rent that comes from taxes and the related contractual agreements.

Because of weak institutions, such as parliament, the judiciary and the ombudsman in these countries, income from minerals ends up in the foreign accounts of the men and women in high office; it is rarely used to propel economic growth at home. This has sometimes sparked tension and conflict on a national scale. In fact, fighting over the share of the national wealth has been one of the key causes of internal conflicts. And, in most cases, failed leaders and looters usually use conflict between ethnic groups as a basis for avoiding accountability.

The paradox of oil

Oil discovery should be a blessing to host countries. In the case of Africa, however, especially given what has happened in Nigeria as a socio-economic consequence of its oil reserves (internal strife, conflicts, calls for the secession of the Niger Delta region, and a great deal of corruption), most observers think that it has turned into a curse.

The oil sector contributes a lot to economic growth in some sub-Saharan countries. In terms of the share of oil in overall GDP, oil contributes around 45 per cent of Angola's national GDP; 69 per cent in the Republic of Congo; 37 per cent in Chad; 57 per cent in Equatorial Guinea; and around 30 per cent in Nigeria (2010 figures) (Takebe & York, 2011). Oil contributes to export receipts. In sub-Saharan Africa, oil-exporting countries are Angola, Cameroon, Chad, Republic of Congo, Côte d'Ivoire, Equatorial Guinea, Gabon and Nigeria. All the other African countries are net oil importers.

If the revenues from oil were managed well, they would have helped government to provide good roads and modernise rail transport, establish healthcare facilities, create support programmes for universal education and modernise agriculture.

Oil sector revenue as a portion of overall GDP, 2005 and 2010

	2005 (%)	2010 (%)
Angola	62.0	45.3
Cameroon	8.4	6.1
Chad	46.8	36.9
Republic of Congo	64.1	69.4
Côte d'Ivoire	2.7	1.8
Equatorial Guinea	82.6	57.4
Gabon	51.8	46.7
Nigeria	38.4	29.1

Source: Takebe, M. &. York, R.C., 2011. External sustainability of oil-producing sub-Saharan African countries. IMF Working Paper, WP/11/207. August 2011, http://www.imf.org/external/pubs/ft/wp/2011/wp11207.pdf (accessed on 25 January 2012)

Note: Ghana started producing oil in 2010; figures are not yet available.

In Uganda, when oil was discovered, prayers were organised by the highest national authorities.[4] This shows the importance attached to oil discovery in that country. At the time of writing, a special military oil protection unit had been recruited because of the sensitivity of the oil project. The leadership was aware of the challenges that Nigeria faced. Professor Paul Collier, an economist at Oxford University, and an authority on oil in Africa, cautioned Uganda about the need for better oil management.

Leaders in Uganda reasoned that agriculture, the mainstay of the economy, had not yielded enough money to generate sustained economic growth and reduce poverty. Most of their hopes rested on oil.

Nations that discover oil need to do a few things differently. Governments need to train people to equip them to manage the oil sector and oil-related industries. Management of this sector would do better with less interference from politicians. Government should limit itself to establishing relevant institutions, such as petroleum and gas facilitation authorities. It is also necessary that governments pass laws to regulate the sector. Legislation to oversee petroleum and gas revenue is also needed; this could be achieved through amendment of these countries' existing income tax laws.

Equally important is the need for expertise in negotiating production sharing agreements. The private sector's interest is profit. Governments must ensure, however, that the national interest prevails through oil revenue sharing agreements, taxes, employment of citizens and provision of goods and services that the sector needs. The economic benefits of oil extraction are mainly in two forms: income in the form of capital and labour, and rents to government, which can be spent on infrastructure, health, education and other vital sectors. In low-income countries, such as Ghana or Uganda, the economic returns via capital and employment will be minimal because of the level of capital development and relevant education and qualifications needed (e.g. oil engineers, oil lawyers, oil value chain specialists, etc.). Consequently, qualified overseas professionals are more likely to benefit from labour and capital. So the governments in these countries need to manage rents well in order to benefit their own citizens. These minerals get depleted – they are not a renewable resource. Oil deposits in Libya, for instance, will be depleted in about 40 years, so future generations in Libya will no longer benefit from oil wealth.

Government's failure to understand its role would render oil discovery and extraction in countries like Ghana and Uganda a curse.

Can Africa achieve meaningful cooperation over its resources?
Although it is not yet possible to foresee an African federal system like that of the US, Africa nevertheless needs to enhance inter-state cooperation. Attempts to create a united African state that brings together all the African states in one political federation have not been successful so far. There is a need for an arrange-

ment by which all African states can collectively and meaningfully discuss the continent's development, be it economic, social or political.[5] On the agenda should be growth, poverty, disease and conflict. The latter affects economic growth because the affected country and its neighbours lose business and revenue.

During the time of the Organisation of African Unity (OAU), wars and conflicts continued unabated. And the organisation that replaced the OAU, the African Union (AU), has also failed to deliver because of personal, regional and external interests.

There are two forces that militate against African unity: externally from US and the EU; and the internal forces being pushed by the powerful power brokers in parts of Africa. There is much doubt in the minds of the powerful external forces about what a united Africa might become. They are unsure whether Africa is likely to become a stronger player in geopolitical terms, competing with the US and EU, where it has previously been a 'begging bowl'; or whether, like before, it may ally with Russia or forge a stronger partnership with China (often regarded by the US and UK as undemocratic but nonetheless a useful trade partner).

Internally, do individual African heads of state want a 'United States of Africa'? The answer is no because unity is not in the interest of these individual heads of state. Having failed to create a strong inter-state union because of disagreements among key leaders in East Africa, South Africa and Libya, other African nations have opted for and now support regional entities, such as the East African Community (EAC), Southern African Development Community (SADC), Economic Community of West Africa (ECOWAS) and Economic Community of Central African States (ECCAS). This has deprived Africa of the opportunity to work towards a single united continental entity. Lack of African cooperation has meant that every country faces global challenges alone, and this has been counterproductive. Individually, small countries cannot address the immense challenges posed by global powers.

The failure to achieve this elusive pan-African cooperation may have to do with how people understand and define the term 'African'. People in Egypt or Sudan define themselves not as Africans, but as Arabs. There are those in Africa who view themselves first and foremost as Indians. What about Mauritians? And do white people of European descent in South Africa refer to themselves as African? There is an urgent need to find answers to these questions. The long civil war in southern Sudan was mainly about subjugation of blacks by Arabs, who are predominantly in the north. People in the south are black and mainly Christian.

It is ironic that the May 2011 meeting to discuss the future of Libya took place in London without the participation of the AU and key regional leaders from Africa. This reflects the sentiment that the EU and the US do not regard Arab Africa as part of the African continent, but site it more in the context of the Middle East.

Former President Mbeki[6] of South Africa, who was involved in negotiating a peace agreement in Libya, said that lack of continental cohesion had done little to fend off developed countries from dominating Africa – even to the extent of ignoring the role of the AU in negotiating peace on the continent. He has said that African governments lack a common stance in terms of dealing with Western powers' intervention in Africa. He said that African countries need to work together under a continental arrangement. He asserted that this apparent lack of cohesion has meant that Africa has failed to defend itself against Western powers' 'violent interventions'[7] in their quest for global dominance.

However, Africa will only realise tangible development dividends if its inhabitants put less emphasis on the colour of their skin (and their origins during the migration era). Anyone who is a citizen of Africa should regard themselves as African, regardless of where they came from. Or maybe we should adopt South African revolutionary Steve Biko's[8] approach. Biko viewed black not as a colour, but as an experience; and if you are oppressed, you are black.

America is a good example of a country united in its diversity and working collectively towards the progress of the nation. Citizens from that country literally originate from every part of the world.

Impromptu discussions with Africans within the continent and in the diaspora reveal, at times justifiably, that some of them wish they belonged elsewhere.[9] There is little wonder that many people who earn money in Africa choose to bank it outside the continent. In some cases, of course, such as conflict zones, this is a justifiable measure to avoid risk.

Effect of corruption on economic growth and development

According to late President Mwanawasa of Zambia, 'the impact of corruption is ghastly if not contained . . . Left uncontained, corruption threatens to undermine the credibility of government, and the very existence of Zambia as a nation. Therefore it is not HIV/AIDS, it is not poverty, but corruption, which poses the greatest threat to our people and nation.' (Henriot 2007: 3).

Whenever you discuss corruption, which is rampant in Africa, it will be argued that corruption does not only occur in Africa. But what is the effect of corruption in Africa in comparison to what happens elsewhere? And how should one define corruption? This is a moot point. The IMF defines it as 'abuse of authority or trust for private benefit . . . a temptation indulged in not only by public officials but also by those in positions of trust or authority in private enterprises or non-profit organisations'. (IMF, 2000)

Rather than providing a universal definition, the United Nations Convention Against Corruption simply proposes a comprehensive set of standards, measures and rules that all countries can apply in order to strengthen their legal and regulatory regimes to fight corruption. It also calls for preventive measures and the criminalisation of the most prevalent forms of corruption in both public and private sectors. The most prevalent forms of corruption may include bribery, fraud, embezzlement, extortion, nepotism and influence peddling, and cronyism. The list also includes the appropriation of public property or assets for private use. In

Nigeria, under the Corrupt Practices and Other Related Offences Act of 2000, 'corruption includes bribery, fraud and other related offences'. According to Justice Emmanuel Olayinka Ayoola, chairman of the Independent Corrupt Practices Commission, 'the commonest form of corruption in Nigeria used to be bribery but in recent years this has been overtaken in level of prevalence by embezzlement and theft from public funds, extortion, abuse of discretion, abuse of public power for private gain, favouritism and nepotism, conflict of interest and illegal political party financing'.

In other African countries, such as Zambia, corruption has been described as the 'fifth component' in a productive economy – after profits, wages, rent and interest. The Nyanja term 'Nchekeleko' means 'give me my share' or 'cut me a piece'. It is a common word in Zambia's offices. The same is happening, however, in Nigeria, Uganda, Kenya and Zambia (to mention but a few).

Political corruption in sub-Saharan Africa

No less than 40 per cent of African savings are held in offshore accounts outside the continent, equivalent to $700–800 billion. In Asia the rate is 3–6 per cent (Lerrick, 2005). The commonly held view in Africa is that ill-gotten money from corrupt practices is usually kept far away from the country from which it has been stolen. The corrupt African leaders have kept their money in offshore banks. Only a small portion of it is money genuinely invested overseas.

The World Bank has documented the damaging effect of corruption on economic growth, especially in Africa. It has noted that corruption hinders economic growth and development by discouraging investment and diverting funds meant for infrastructure into other things. It adds that it undermines social development efforts by diverting or even draining the available resources (which are usually scarce) – hence health centres that are short of medicine and schools with no equipment needed for teaching. Corruption also hinders political development, preventing free and fair elections and ushering poor leaders into office.

A story has been told of an official in an East African country who demanded from a contractor a bribe equivalent to the value of two layers of road tarmac in order to win the tender for constructing a road. The road should have been built with no fewer than four layers. Financially constrained, the contractor was forced to construct the road with only two layers. The effects of this kind of corruption are various. First, you will have poor-quality roads, which have to be replaced after a short period. It also means limiting the carriage of goods on trucks transported on this road to the markets; loss of lives and goods; and a bigger medical bill. None of these deterred the official from obtaining the kickback he wanted.

In June 2007, the World Bank and the UN Office on Drugs and Crime (UNODC) published a report on stolen assets, estimating that 25 per cent of the GDP of African states are lost to corruption each year. The total amounts to around $148 billion per year. The *Global Corruption Report 2004*, published by Transparency International, identified Mobutu, who ruled the then Zaire from 1965 to 1997, and Sani Abacha, the kleptocratic president of Nigeria from 1993 and 1998, to be the top looters of public funds in Africa. Mobuto is estimated to have stolen funds amounting to $5 billion,[1] while Abacha is estimated to have pillaged between $2 billion and $5 billion. These are just two examples of African leaders after independence.

Corruption Perception Index 2011

This index measures the public's perceptions of corruption in a country. The index assigns nations a scale from 10 (highly clean)

75

to 0 (highly corrupt). Except for Botswana, which is rated fairly clean, almost all the countries in the sub-Saharan region rate poorly on the index. More than 28 countries rate below 3; Mauritius (at 5.1) and Rwanda (at 5.0) are at the middle point of the index; Namibia and South Africa are around 4 (Transparency International, 2011).

Countries obtain revenues from exports, investments, taxes and levies, among others. In most African countries, however, bribery and kickbacks help businesspeople escape taxes and customs charges. Yet customs dues bring in revenues for most import-dependent countries. Corruption, therefore, causes big losses to the growth and development of African countries. It is a leakage in the state's financial mechanism for generating national revenue to invest in infrastructure and social development. Corruption has been estimated to increase the cost of goods and services by around 10 per cent and reduce government tax revenues by as much as 50 per cent.[2] It is difficult to accurately tally the amount of stolen dollars stashed away in private offshore accounts by the corrupt in Africa. At the low end, former British Prime Minister Blair's Commission for Africa believes the sum to be $95 billion, or the equivalent of more than half of poor Africa's external debt. Others, however, estimate the amount at more than $500 billion (Lerrick, 2005). In Nigeria alone, in 2006, the head of Nigeria's Economic and Financial Crimes Commission, Nuhu Ribadu, estimated that the country lost some $380 billion to corruption between independence in 1960 and the end of military rule in 1999 (quoted in Ogundiya, 2010). According to Blair, this amount is equivalent to all the Western aid given to Africa in almost four decades, and equivalent to 300 years of British aid for the continent (Ogundiya, 2010). It is also said to be six times the US aid given to post-war Europe under the Marshall Plan.

In 2002, Professor Ayittey of the American University in Washington listed the personal wealth of 12 African heads of state. Of these, the lowest figure was $3 million. Five of the leaders had amassed between $2 billion and $20 billion. General Sani Abacha of Nigeria had an estimated fortune of $20 billion. One can therefore say that, disregarding morality, it certainly pays to be a president in Africa.

Corrupt leaders in Africa and their personal wealth

LEADER	COUNTRY	ESTIMATED PLUNDER
1. General Sani Abacha	Nigeria	$20 billion
2. President Boigny	Ivory Coast	$6 billion
3. General Ibrahim Babangida	Nigeria	$5 billion
4. President Mobutu	Zaire	$4 billion
5. President Mouza Traore	Mali	$2 billion
6. Teodoro Obiang Nguema Mbasogo	Equatorial Guinea	Approx. $600 million
7. President Henri Bedie	Ivory Coast	$300 million
8. President Denis Nguesso	Congo	$200 million
9. President Paul Biya	Cameroon	$200 million
10. President Omar Bongo	Gabon	$80 million
11. President Haile Mariam	Ethiopia	$30 million
12. President Hissene Habre	Chad	$3 million

Sources: Gbenga, L., 2007. Corruption and development in Africa: Challenges for political and economic change. *Humanity & Social Sciences Journal* 2(1): 1–7; Ayittey, G., 2010. The worst of the worst. *Foreign Policy*, July/August 2010; Ayittey, G., 2010. The worst of the worst revisited. *Foreign Policy*, 9 September 2011

In Africa corruption is rampant. Politicians and other leaders have lost all sense of shame with regard to misuse and theft of public assets. Rumours abound of presidents, prime ministers, ministers

and senior army officers who sold off the state's public enterprises at a small fee, either directly to themselves or to others, and
bought them back immediately after the sale. This occurred during the privatisation phases of most African economies. No wonder that most public enterprises that were sold in these countries
collapsed. They were given to those who knew nothing about business practices. Many sold off the assets and were left with nothing
more than the business's certificate of registration.

It should come as no surprise then, than when defeated in elections, many incumbents refuse to hand over power. In recent
times, from Zimbabwe to Kenya to Ivory Coast, leaders have supposedly been defeated at the polls, but have refused to hand over
power. Instead, they are hastily sworn in, entering into bloody con-
frontation and later power-sharing deals. Incumbents often fear,
and indeed with good reason, that once they leave office, legal
proceedings might begin against them.

Flawed procurement

Often government property is misused or sold without proper
accountability. This practice is not limited to politicians, but also
includes civil servants who belong to the 'eating group'. They establish companies and supply to governments at inflated prices.
This means that the beneficiaries of government services, the
citizens, receive poorer service and support in exchange for a
bigger fee. The procurement processes, whether funded by government or the World Bank, are flawed. When preparing specifi-
cations, government officials make them in a way that favours
particular suppliers. This is usually unknown to the donors who
fund certain projects. Another form of corruption can be found
in the so-called prequalified list. The government will call for
suppliers to be prequalified. Once the list is made, the government agency gets the chance to invite the same companies it

wants to 'eat with'. Once they have prequalified, the agency is required to send bid documents to at least three suppliers/contractors on the prequalified list. This is an accepted way of tendering, employed by government agencies and other entities.

Overcoming corruption in Africa

As mentioned, the late Zambian President Levy Mwanawasa once remarked that it is corruption that poses the greatest threat to the people. The threat of corruption should never be taken lightly. If not addressed rigorously, it can jeopardise the very existence of a nation and result in the loss of many lives.

Political will is needed to fight corruption, which, according to studies, consumes more than 20 per cent of several African countries' national budgets. This is no small loss. Opposition politicians and governments of developed countries have begun to propose regime change as a way of ending corruption and bad governance. This is not a panacea, however. Regime change with a reformist government will not stop corruption in itself. After all, in Africa, we have seen people sell their homes to fund campaigns for political office or a parliamentary seat. It is unlikely that such individuals will have the motivation to fight corruption. Where will they get the money to replace the house they sold? And it would be even more difficult to send home all the government employees and politicians and start from a clean plate.

There are two productive ways to overcome corruption: firstly, establishing laws to effectively address the vice and, secondly, the enforcement of these laws. By law, all public servants should declare their wealth at the start of their term of service and then periodically thereafter. Public servants must become accountable by law to the public for their wealth, their property and their business interests. Anti-money-laundering laws are also important in the fight against corruption. The process of restricting corruption needs to start by making it illegal to transfer fraudulently obtained finances to foreign accounts.[3]

It is important that these laws are enforced. Governments have the duty to support and empower the institutions that fight corruption (police, judiciary, ombudsman and parliamentary legislature). This can be done by giving them political support, ample resources and personnel skills. Governments should also establish anti-corruption courts specifically to handle cases related to corruption. Corruption cases should stop being tried in the criminal courts: they must not be treated as normal criminal or civil cases.

The anti-corruption courts should be independent of the executive branch of government and apply punitive measures that leave offenders limited chances of appeal. These courts should also have the power to apply the principle of the time value of money. This means that the court should be able to recover from the offender the stolen money with interest, taking into account the time period the offender has been using the assets or money obtained through corrupt practice. For example, if an offender stole $100, they should refund the principal plus interest calculated over the number of years the money was embezzled. They should also be charged a higher rate of interest than the normal rate imposed on those borrowing from banks to invest and create wealth.

Establishing anti-corruption courts and laws is not enough per se: there is also a need for an appropriate level of punishment to fit the crime.[4] African governments have to make corruption a risky, expensive and unattractive undertaking so as to transform the continent.[5] Corruption should be punished in the same way as serious, offensive crimes, such as murder. In the long run, governments that do not put in place measures and laws to enforce anti-corruption will be dead in the water. To use Keynes's words, corruption can result in the removal of the government in power through various means, including military coups. Governments should avoid glib, empty statements and sloganeering when it comes to tackling corruption, but ensure that there is zero tolerance of corruption, backed by firm commitment and action.

Governments should act swiftly to get back the money stolen through corrupt activities and use it to build essential infrastructure, such as roads, provide much-needed health centres and promote trade. Fortunately, governments in Europe, where looted money is often stashed, are starting to cooperate with these endeavours.

Corruption thrives where accountability is weak. African governments need strong institutions to fight this evil. It all begins with strong political leadership, which can play a decisive role in preventing it. Another important law that can help governments obtain information about this vice is enacting what can be termed the 'whistle blower's act', designed to protect those who expose corruption. There should be strategies intended to make reporting corruption attractive, with financial rewards as a recompense for the risks faced by those who report it.

Most donor money is wasted via corruption. Aid money has contributed a great deal to the escalation of corruption. It is necessary and urgent that those who give aid rethink this policy. Alternatively, until African countries stop receiving aid, donors must play an active part in ending corruption. Any sign of corruption should result in immediate withdrawal of support by donors. This has two advantages. Firstly, the governments receiving aid will be forced to act, and, secondly, they will rethink aid.

Role of the media in fighting corruption

The media is a vital tool for exposing and fighting corruption. Once the corrupt are exposed by the media, they have nowhere to hide. Sometimes, government inspectors have used journalists to investigate errant public officials. Unfortunately, however, like their brothers in government, some media organisations have shown signs of unethical practices. Stories abound of editors who are bribed to drop important stories about key public officials. Publishing executives, who 'dine' with public officials, often refuse, under the umbrella of editorial policy, to publish critical articles on corruption involving senior public servants and politicians. Those journalists who refuse to be gagged are expelled.

Population strategies and educating the people

*'I will continue making as many babies as
long as my relatives are there to take care of them.
What are relatives for anyway?'*
(Tabaire, 2011)

There are divergent opinions regarding the consequences of population growth on economic development. Whereas some view rapid population growth as a serious problem, others instead assert that it is positive for growth. International evidence on the relationship between rapid population growth and economic growth is inconsistent because the underlying parameters and assumptions vary in different countries, depending, among other factors, on the country's level of development and the 'quality' of the population. In development studies, 'quality' of population can be defined in terms of levels of health, education and income. For the sub-Saharan countries, which have a disease burden and high mortality rates, and where growth and productivity depend on human labour, the size of the population is important.

At the family level in this region, however, more children mean more poverty – as many large families cannot afford quality education, healthcare and even food. So there is a positive correlation between the size of the family and its level of poverty in the region; a large family is a threat to its survival. It is ironic that poor families tend to have more children.

Since the late 1980s, Africa has witnessed the problem of a growing population segment of young people. To give the demographic example of two countries, half of the population of Ghana and Uganda is below the age of 18. This is an economically dependent group, which hampers economic growth. Young people need food, shelter, clothing, healthcare and education, which are all costs.

According to the *Economic Report on Africa 2010*, Africa's population, despite disease-related fatality (e.g. HIV/AIDS and malaria), increased by 2.3 per cent between 2008 and 2009 (UNECA, 2010), and reached about 1 billion in 2011 (African Economic Outlook, 2011). Top of the list of countries with the highest population growth rates in the world are Liberia (4.6 per cent), Niger (4.3 per cent), Burkina Faso (3.7 per cent) and Uganda (3.2 per cent) (UBOS, 2009).

There are various reasons for the high growth rates. First, there is the traditional African view of children as contributors or sources of wealth. In cultures that believe in dowry or bride price, the more females a family produces, the greater the family's wealth when the girls are married off. And the boys can be employed to work the land and find food.

At the national level, however, high population growth rates are likely to cause problems associated with population density (population per square kilometre), such as land fragmentation, soil erosion due to over-farming the land and land conflict, among others. With increasing population density, less land is available for agriculture. High population densities threaten rural families' traditional means of subsistence. This is exacerbated when a smaller portion of a country's land is not arable in the first place, such as mountainous areas.

But there is another reason for the demand for more children in Africa: insurance. Families produce more children not only because they will till the earth or bring dowries, but in the event that disease claims the lives of some children, others will be available to provide for their ageing parents. This practice was no different in the pre-industrial societies of Europe and Japan.

Population growth in Africa is also a natural outcome of lack of economic opportunity and empowerment, especially on the part of women. Women are not given equal education opportunities; they have an imposed inferior status in African societies; they lack assets to generate wealth and are dependent on their husbands. Their role is manifested in their ability to go on producing children.

There are disagreements among politicians, economists, demographers and the development experts on the effect of a high population growth rate on a state's economic growth path. Some leaders in Africa support the need for large populations. What is interesting, though, is that the same leaders may well have few children themselves and do not encourage their children to produce more grandchildren for them.

Having more children may be linked to the African culture of entrenched patriarchal values, a culture divided along gender lines. African women are expected to produce children. In Africa today, it is not uncommon to find a family of 15 or more children from the same father. When families produce lots of children, this increases the number of mouths to feed – and hence population growth.

Since well before European intervention and the arrival of Christianity and Islam in Africa, African men have practised polygamy. The role of the fertile female in traditional (and modern) African cultures is central to African society's core values – to be able to produce offspring is a self-defining feature of womankind in African culture and a celebration of womanhood. The family rejoices with childbirth and the extended African family supports the children. Morrell et al. (2011) emphasise the importance of motherhood. They put it that motherhood gives women strength and value (Morrell, Bhana & Shefer, 2011).

Religion also has a role to play in the population agenda. When the new religions of Christianity and Islam were introduced in Africa, the view towards more children did not change. Orthodox Christianity and Islam strongly oppose family-planning methods.

Christians believe that producing children is doing God's work of procreation. What they may not critically consider is that the numbers of offspring should be in line with the family's means to support them. In Africa Muslims have the privilege (and often they present it as a religious right) of having four wives loving them equally. Although Catholics are not permitted by the church to divorce, it does not help from an economic perspective when they strongly oppose modern family-planning methods. Discouraging family planning indirectly encourages big families, and very large families cannot be supported by the poor.

Again in Africa, even some Christians who have wed in church go ahead and marry more wives and produce more children out of wedlock.

The Asian tiger countries that have realised high economic growth rates and greatly reduced absolute poverty among the population had similar religions that are practised in Africa. So how come they did not produce 20 children or marry four wives and produce more? This is explained by the African culture of love for children. But since culture is associated with the economics of society, we can continue to argue that more children were seen as an investment (dowry from the girls and farming by the boys).

Population and health, education and employability

China has promoted a one-child per family policy for quite some time. And in Hong Kong, Taiwan and Singapore there tend to be few children per family. Chile provides a good example of the relationship between population growth and economic growth. Chile experienced a dramatic fertility-rate drop from an average of 5.3 children in 1950 to 2.3 in 2000. Chile's economic development improved over the same period.

Population growth is significant both in terms of the number of workers and consumers. However, it is not just the numbers that matter in the labour force, but also productivity per person, and consumers' purchasing power parity. Productivity per person depends on the quality of the labour force (i.e. skills and qualifications), technological progress, and the levels of capital deepening and capital widening, among others. More than ever, Africa needs quality labour to ensure quality and quantity of output, and create demand as consumers for a country's products. Such labour requires particular skills, qualifications and education. Therefore, countries need to devise policies that gear their economies towards growth, given the size of the population and the quality of the labour force. Campaigns on the relationship between a quality population, wealth creation and purchasing power parity should be led by government.

The table shows that in 2010, more than 25 countries in Africa had high population growth rates close to or above 3 per cent, and most of them with a fertility rate of above four. (Fertility rate is the average number of children per woman.)

Demographic indicators for Africa

	Total population (1000s) (2010)	Population growth rate (%) (2005–2010)	Infant mortality rate (per 1 000) (2010)	Total fertility rate (per woman) (2010)
Angola	18,993	2.9	110.9	5.5
Benin	9,212	3.4	80.8	5.3
Burkina Faso	16,287	3.7	77.8	5.8
Burundi	8,519	3.1	94.6	4.3
Chad	11,506	3.0	127.0	6.0
DRC	67,827	3.0	113.9	5.8
Equatorial Guinea	693	2.8	95.4	5.2

	Total population (1000s) (2010)	Population growth rate (%) (2005–2010)	Infant mortality rate (per 1 000) (2010)	Total fertility rate (per woman) (2010)
Eritrea	5,224	3.4	51.0	4.4
Ethiopia	84,976	2.8	74.9	5.1
Gambia	1,751	2.9	74.0	4.9
Kenya	40,863	2.8	60.4	4.8
Liberia	4,102	4.6	91.3	4.9
Madagascar	20,146	2.9	61.0	4.5
Malawi	15,692	3.0	78.4	5.4
Mali	13,323	2.5	102.9	5.3
Mauritania	3,366	2.9	102.9	2.5
Mozambique	23,406	2.8	94.9	2.5
Niger	15,891	4.3	83.7	7.0
Nigeria	158,259	2.5	106.6	5.1
Rwanda	10,277	2.9	95.9	5.3
Senegal	12,861	2.8	57.0	4.8
Sierra Leone	5,836	2.9	101.5	5.1
Tanzania	45,040	3.1	59.8	5.5
Togo	6,780	2.6	68.3	4.1
Uganda	33,796	3.2	70.3	6.7
Zambia	13,257	2.6	86.5	5.6
Africa	**1,031,472**	**2.4**	**78.6**	**4.4**

Sources: African Economic Outlook. Available at: http://www.africaneconomic-outlook.org/en/data-statistics/ (accessed on 23 January 2012); UBOS, Statistical Abstract 2009

Land fragmentation problems in Africa are associated with high population growth rate. More children inherit small plots of land from their parents. The small plots of land do not support productive commercial agriculture.

Land tenure systems in sub-Saharan Africa also have an effect on rapid population growth. In most communities in the region, land belongs to the whole clan and families cultivate it together. The land one family has cultivated can be literally regarded as their land – though they may not have legal title to it. This is the case in Rwanda, Uganda, Tanzania, Kenya, South Sudan and Sudan, as well as in several other sub-Saharan African countries. So families may need more members in order to cultivate a large piece of land that they can claim from the clan. The fewer people the family has, the smaller the chances of claiming a larger portion of the communal land.

Economic growth and health

Which should come first: better health or more income? Economists and demographers Bloom and Canning (2000) in their article 'The health and wealth of nations' say that although a positive correlation between health and income per capita is one of the best-known relationships in development, there has emerged another view about health and income per capita. The original relationship indicated that higher levels of income result in better health, as those with a good income can afford a healthier lifestyle and better access to healthcare. The new and intriguing possibility, however, is that better health instead results in greater income.

Bloom and Canning give four reasons to support this view: a healthy population tends to have higher labour productivity; healthier people who live longer tend to invest in skills development; improvement in longevity tends to create a greater savings culture for retirement; and when infant and child mortality rates decline, fertility also declines because families know their children will live, hence income per capita rises. The latter is referred to as the 'demographic dividend' (Bloom, Canning & Sevilla, 2003).[1]

According to the World Health Organization (WHO, 2001), the health status of the population, as measured by life expectancy, is a significant determinant or predictor of future economic growth.

Bloom and Canning (2000), based on various studies comparing two countries at the same level but with one of them having a five-year advantage in life expectancy, conclude that the income per capita in the healthier country will grow at 0.3–0.5 per cent per year more than its less healthy counterpart.

Improvements in health have been recognised as one of the major pillars for East Asia's economic miracle.[2] Unfortunately for sub-Saharan Africa, where a disease burden has induced families to produce more children due to high mortality, and resources have to be shared among a large number of children, economic growth has been suppressed.

A healthy populace will save and invest for the future because they hope to live longer, so it can be concluded that a healthy population is a key factor for economic growth.

Since independence, average life expectancy in sub-Saharan Africa has been between 30 and 40 years, and the population growth rate has been around 3 per cent. Something is wrong here. On average, people have been dying before reaching their 40s – their most productive years. This has a negative effect on the way people in the region behave – it makes people think on a short-term basis and it discourages investment.

The only option for governments now remains to invest in better health services and the provision of basic education by the state to those who cannot afford it.[3] The health and skills of the population are very important to their contribution to personal wealth, income, employment, innovation and overall economic growth. This book supports these endeavours.

Economic growth and population control

As the need for wealth increases, the demand for children tends to decrease. This is usually supported by population-control measures. The developed countries realised the importance of managed population numbers and have benefited economically. The US has a GDP of $15 094 billion[4] and a population of 308.7 million (US Census Bureau, 2010[5]). The US population is growing slowly, with a fertility rate of 2.1. Although sub-Saharan Africa is geographically larger than the US and although Africa occupies more than 20 per cent of the world's land area, this is no excuse for continued rapid population growth. Africa's population (around one-sixth of the world's total population) is around 1 billion compared with the US population of 308 million. However, the entire African continent's GDP is just $1 150 billion, or 0.0076 per cent of US GDP. This is no mere accident. The US has undergone a long period of planning and sustained growth. And China, which has a big population, achieved economic progress through a deliberate policy of population control – the one-child policy.[6] More than 30 years ago, China launched this population-control policy, credited with cutting its population growth to an all-time low and simultaneously contributing to two decades of immense economic development. Like all other policies aimed at enhancing economic growth, however, there are costs associated with the policy: China has a disproportionately large number of elderly people; a disproportionately high number of male births attributable to sex-selective abortions; increased female infant and child mortality rates; and the collapse of a credible government birth reporting system.

As discussed earlier, with a healthy population, infant and child mortality rates decline. Women's fertility also declines because people know their children will live and grow, hence the demand for children falls. Population-control measures by government and family-planning efforts by individual families ensue. In pre-industrialised Japan, the onset of the industrial era was preceded by 150 years of very slow population growth, which allowed family incomes to increase faster than population growth. This population growth level was influenced by the government.[7] To have a quality labour force and a generally healthy population requires economic planning. It requires that a country knows what resources it has, how to transform those resources into finished products and what number of people such an economy can support with the resources. An economy has to achieve a balance between the number of people at a given time and its national wealth. As Michael Fairbanks said while in Rwanda, prosperity is a choice,[8] and if it is a choice, then when you choose it you have to work to ensure that you prosper. Deliberate decisions and choices have to be made. China has had the one-child policy and African countries would do well to borrow from this example.

Population growth and government expenditure

Economic growth and development planning ignore population management policies at their peril. In their objective of achieving the Millennium Development Goal (MDG)[9] of universal education, several countries in the sub-Saharan region have Universal Primary Education (UPE) and Universal Post-Primary Education and Training (UPPET) or Universal Secondary Education (USE) programmes, which are good strategies to enhance human capital for production and growth. However, if these countries do not plan how to manage their populations, they will experience a dependency burden (the ratio of dependent young and old people to the working age group).[10] They will then have a problem with their national budgets. The disproportionate amount of funds allocated to the primary and secondary school-going age group (with an average of 4.4 children per family in Africa) will put a financial strain on infrastructure and healthcare.

In 2010, the age dependency ratio (i.e. the ratio between the working-age and dependent segments) for sub-Saharan Africa was nearly 1.6 times higher than the world average – 85 per cent as opposed to 54 per cent (World Bank, 2011). The population of the region is young: 43 per cent were under the age of 15 in 2010 and it was growing fast, with an estimated growth rate of 2.4 per cent between 2005 and 2010 (UNESCO, 2011). This means that there is a larger than average proportion of people who do not work but depend on the labour of the few. This is not good for economic growth, which is fuelled by the quantitative increase in goods and services. These goods and services require markets, buyers with demand. Those who do not earn by necessity depend on others for their survival.

Education and training for wealth creation

'Education is the only way out; the way out of ignorance;
the way out of darkness; into the glorious light.'
 (The Great Debaters, 2007)

'A nation can never be ignorant and free.'
 (Thomas Jefferson, quoted in Time, *26 June 2006)*

In order to develop Africa's economies, it is necessary to develop skill sets to enhance productivity and competitiveness at both the corporate and national levels. There are numerous factors that determine a nation's competitiveness. However, according to the *Global Competitiveness Report 2011–2012*, the World Economic Forum has identified 12 determinants of especial significance for Africa: institutions, infrastructure, macroeconomic stability, health and primary education, higher education and training, market efficiency, labour market efficiency, financial market sophistication, technology readiness, market size, business sophistication and innovation.

During colonialism, there was a practice of selecting collaborators' children and sending them to Europe, mainly Britain and France, to train them how to use 'correct' European table manners and etiquette. These courses were not relevant to the needs of Africa's development during and after colonialism. Most of the graduates of these courses did not return to help develop the continent. Today, children should be encouraged to leave Africa and study subjects overseas related to enhancing economic growth. Scholarships must consider the importance of subjects and skill sets that will enhance Africa's development. Asian countries have tended to offer courses specifically focused on industrial and economic development.

The Asian Development Bank has identified education and training as one of the factors responsible for Asia's corporate competitiveness. At one time, Ghana and Uganda had the same level of economic growth and per capita income as South Korea. In fact, some literature shows that Uganda and Ghana were slightly better off than South Korea. They were rich in natural resources. Today, however, South Korea supports Ghana and Uganda with aid. One of the reasons for the turnaround is that Asian countries, South Korea being no exception, developed relevant education and training. Africans placed greater emphasis on more liberal arts (humanities) disciplines and left mathematics and engineering sciences to the Asians (William, 2006).

This situation has not changed. But it will certainly have to change if countries are interested in innovation and value addition.[11] The UN Economic Commission for Africa (UNECA) Report points out that although literacy rates have improved, the challenge is for African education systems to produce graduates with skill sets that are necessary to develop their economies. The report also notes that gross enrolment ratios in secondary and tertiary education are very low compared with those of other regions of the world, and graduates are less trained in appropriate skills.

According to the *African Youth Report 2011*, most African countries still continue to put more emphasis on the provision of basic education in order to achieve the MDG of UPE (UNECA, 2011). However, this will not in itself generate growth and create jobs for the youth in Africa. They require skills that need to be acquired through education and training beyond UPE level. Post-primary education is important. Tertiary education is needed to absorb those who finish UPE and create job makers, not job seekers. The findings of research conducted by the UNESCO Institute for Statistics are revealing. It found that of gross enrolment ratios in tertiary education for selected countries in the region, Algeria and Mauritius were among the countries with the highest enrolment of the official school-age population in tertiary institutions, at 31 and 26 per cent respectively in 2009. This research also found that those countries that were very successful in UPE, such as Uganda, had very low tertiary enrolment, at 4 per cent. Even Zimbabwe, with its high literacy rate, reported only 3 per cent total tertiary enrolment (UNECA, 2011).

Does Africa inherently lack the relevant disciplines at the tertiary level, or is there a human-resources capacity crisis? This is a subject that has been debated a great deal, with some researchers and national leaders saying that the problem is not necessarily a lack of an educated labour force, but the brain drain happening on the continent, with skilled people emigrating, mainly to the US and Europe. This does not, however, mean that sub-Saharan Africa should not educate its children. The Chinese are everywhere in the world, but this has not hindered China's rapid growth. Africa needs to create strategies either to train the youth locally or send them to study abroad to acquire the relevant skills and subjects that will lead to development on the continent. And even if there is a brain drain, it is not necessarily negative, as expatriates' remittances are often invested in their home countries.

In conclusion, African countries need to learn from those countries that have achieved economic success through education and training, especially given their higher than average population growth rates. Governments should encourage the study of disciplines that are pertinent to development and value addition in industries such as agriculture, business and IT, which is vital in today's 'global village'. Such training will lead to innovation, quality and quantity of industrial output. This output will generate margins for business, income for the workers and enhance economic growth for the countries.

The informal sector and tools for attracting investment

Most countries in sub-Saharan Africa have a large informal sector and many business relationships are conducted informally.[1] Some studies, including those conducted by the International Labour Organisation (ILO, 2002) and Swedish International Development Agency (SIDA) (Becker, 2004), have estimated the share of non-agricultural employment in the informal workforce at 78 per cent in Africa[2] (compared with 57 per cent in Latin America and the Caribbean, and 45 per cent in Asia). In a study by Friedrich Schneider (2007), a researcher on the informal, or 'shadow', economy, it was found that out of 37 African countries[3] (including Egypt and South Africa), 36 had an informal economy constituting above 30 per cent of the overall economy. Only South Africa had an informal economy below 30 per cent (at 28 per cent). The informal economy in 11 of these countries was 45 per cent and above, with Zimbabwe at 64 per cent, Nigeria at 59 per cent, Tanzania at 58 per cent and the DRC at 50 per cent. So the informal sector in Africa is clearly a significant portion of the economy. For example, a SIDA study reveals that in sub-Saharan Africa, self-employment comprises a greater share of informal employment than wage employment, representing 81 per cent. Although various reasons for the existence of the informal economy[4] have been presented – such as limited absorption of surplus labour, unawareness of government about the contribution of the informal sector, weak formal institutions to provide education and training, structural adjustment programmes, economic hardships and poverty – some writers, such as the renowned Peruvian development economist Hernando de Soto, insist that it is mainly excessive costs, government regulations and corruption in areas such as business start-up, granting of business permits and land titles that have forced people to be tied to the informal sector (De Soto, 2000).

We can say that in most of Africa, the informal economy exists because the government has failed to put in place strategies and programmes to integrate this sector.[5] And no incentives exist to integrate the people working in the informal sector into the mainstream economy, even though the majority of those who work in this sector have qualifications that fit well with the 'real' economy. De Soto (2000) adds that some people are in the informal sector as a rational response to governments' over regulation of micro-entrepreneurs.

There are problems with this informality regarding tax and revenue collection, and growth estimation. First, the government cannot easily estimate annual growth or GDP. Second, when problems arise under such informal relationships, it becomes difficult for the aggrieved parties to get redress in courts of law. Third, it is difficult for government to collect taxes in this sector, and this narrows the tax base for government. This adds to the curse of dependency on foreign aid because governments cannot mobilise revenue domestically. Most states in sub-Saharan Africa have failed to widen their tax base. Their tax revenue contribution to national income or GDP is small.

There are many informal relationships that would otherwise fall under formal business relationships. In Africa, relatives and friends give one another food for free. Such exchanges could, arguably, be classified as the informal economy. Factors of production, such as land, and other assets, such as property and livestock, are often given to friends or relatives for free. This is not good for economic growth. Free exchanges reduce the motivation to work. When such items are given free of charge, the government loses taxes and GDP suffers. In Africa, a lot of tax revenue is not collected because it is in the hands of the informal business community, and in most cases, government then resorts to looking for foreign aid to finance the deficit.

There is an urgent need to formalise the informal sector. Countries cannot develop without knowing the size of their economies. Each country has to know which sectors contribute what and how much. Governments in Africa should establish agencies to study the importance of the informal sector and how to integrate it into the mainstream economy. Strategies include government efforts to grant attractive packages, such as tax benefits, education and training oriented to working in the formal sector. Ultimately, this will be to the benefit of government because, in the long run, it will generate more tax and reduce dependency on aid. It will also help government monitor the flows of businesses and employment, and gain a good estimate of economic growth. Such efforts need to be considered seriously. Goods and services, including employment, should all be traded in a formal, competitive market.

Capital accumulation

By 2005 it was estimated that 1.4 billion people, or a quarter of the population of the developing world, lived below the international poverty line of $1.25 a day at 2005 prices. Progress has been uneven across regions since 1980 to 2010. The poverty rate in East Asia fell from almost 80 per cent to under 20 per cent over this period. By contrast, it stayed at around 50 per cent in sub-Saharan Africa, although there have been signs of progress since the mid-1990s (Shaohua & Martin, 2008). Currently the poverty level in sub-Saharan Africa is on average above 30 per cent. But this figure is still too high. It means that most people live on one meal a day – and most survive from the subsistence economy. Most of the poor live and work in the informal economy.

Capital is very crucial to competitiveness, productivity and economic growth. Michael Porter, Harvard Business School professor, in his book *The Competitive Advantage of Nations* (Porter, 1990) says that the upgrading of an economy requires ample capital to be available at a low real cost and to be allocated efficiently through the banking system and other capital markets to investments with the highest productivity. A low cost of capital not only encourages high levels of investment necessary to improve productivity, but also supports sustained investment by lowering the time discount rate.

Government has a role in influencing the supply and cost of capital, as well as the markets through which it is allocated. Porter points out that providing direct subsidies to firms has been a prominent tool used by governments to attempt to influence factor cost and otherwise shape the competitive advantage of nations. Subsidised capital, subsidised exports and direct grants are employed by nearly every nation in one industry or another. South Korea, like Japan, progressed to the investment-driven stage through a system whereby government borrowed and channelled scarce capital, at subsidised rates, to selected industries.

At the micro-level, or firm level, businesses need to capitalise their investments in order to increase the levels of production, distribution, exports and service delivery. At the national government level, capital is needed for salaries and wages for public servants and consultants, for military and defence purposes and for the construction of infrastructure, etc. There is also a need for money to engage in meaningful economic diplomacy (i.e. seeking trade opportunities and attracting investors).

There are several ways through which governments can raise capital, as opposed to seeking aid. A just and fair engagement in trade remains the most appropriate option. We will deal with this in the following sections.

Create a middle class to enhance economic growth

The middle class is important for economic growth and development. David Landes, an economics historian, in his book *The Wealth and Poverty of Nations* (Landes, 1998) explains that England's move towards industrialisation and growth was due to the presence of 'the great English middle class' of the 18th and 19th centuries.

There are various descriptions of what the middle class is, but without going into the definitions, suffice to say there is enough evidence that if a country wants to enhance and sustain economic growth, then it has to create a middle class.[6] There are several advantages of having a big middle class. The middle classes prefer peace and political stability because they have property or stable jobs that they wish to retain. They prefer to go to court to resolve conflict instead of resorting to violence and mob justice. According to Eduardo Giannetti da Fonseca, one of Brazil's most distinguished economists, the middle classes are 'people who are not resigned to a life of poverty; who are prepared to make sacrifices to create a better life for themselves but who have not started with life's material problems solved because they have material assets to make their lives easy'.[7]

Birdsall, Graham and Pettinato (2000: 1), while defining the middle class as 'the backbone of both the market economy and of democracy in most advanced societies', make a significant point as regards the relevance of a middle class in developing countries. Nancy Birdsall of the Centre for Global Development says that 'the emergence of a middle class . . . is closely associated with growth, and is probably an outcome of growth as much or more than it is an input to growth' (Birdsall, 2010: 2). She suggests that the middle class in developing countries needs to align its economic interests with sound economic policies and good governance, thereby making itself indispensible in processes aimed at achieving sustainable economic growth. She, therefore, defines the middle class in the developing world as including people living on the equivalent of $10 a day or above in 2005. The African Development Bank (AfBD, 2011: 80) defines the African middle class as those with earnings of between $4 and $20 per day. The AfBD says the middle class population –355 million (or 34 per cent of Africa's population) in 2010 – is estimated to rise to 1.1 billion (42 per cent) in 2060.

The middle classes demand such services as banking, insurance and modern healthcare; and they spend money on recreation. All these services are taxed and contribute to government revenue. Above all, they do not need to be told how to plan for their families. They enjoy a lifestyle made available by disposable income and so cannot afford to have more children, who may be a burden on their expenditure and savings. Even in Africa, the middle classes, who mostly live in urban centres, have families that commonly comprise two children. A few extend the number of children to three or four, mainly when they wish to balance the sexes among their children.

Globally, the middle classes, be it in the developed or developing world, share similar characteristics. They provide a market for consumer goods (and are willing to pay a little more for quality). They play a vital role in creating and sustaining democracy (although they cannot do this alone without the rest of the population), as they possess a reasonable amount of discretionary income.[8] The middle classes do not live from hand to mouth, job to job, season to season, as the poor usually do. They usually have a regular income, in most cases through formal employment with a salary and benefits. This class has been viewed conventionally as primarily a source of important inputs for the entrepreneurial sector. They provide labour to investors. They are interested in accumulation of human capital and savings, and this makes them central to the process of capitalist accumulation and a country's growth. The middle class has also been linked to intellectual aspects of society. In 19th-century England, Thomas Malthus (a British political economist, who anticipated grave risks due to over-population and possible food shortages) wrote that 'the middle regions of society seem to be best suited to intellectual improvement'. The basis of his argument is simple: the middle classes can afford to send their children to better schools, and these children end up being future leaders in society. Secondly, unlike the rich, the middle classes of society, while trying to make it in life, work hard and at times innovate due to necessity.

Given the essential characteristics and potential contribution of the middle class, as described above, it is clear that African countries would benefit from a middle class. They need to reach a 'sweet spot of growth',[9] which, according to Homi Kharas of the Brookings Institution, is the point at which the poor start entering the middle class in their millions. This is the point where poor countries, especially in sub-Saharan Africa, can get maximum benefit from their cheap labour, for example, via international trade.

However, caution must be taken to avoid a politically created middle class. This type of middle class does not enhance growth because it changes with the change in the regime that created it. Take, for instance, the situation whereby former rebels in DRC removed Mobutu, or in Uganda where they deposed the Lutwa and Obote governments, or Rwanda, where Kagame's Rwandese Patriotic Front rewarded the fighters and collaborators with lucrative government contracts or jobs in public agencies that pay well, such as revenue agencies. This class will base their wealth and incomes on the survival of the regime in power, and once the regime goes, then that is the demise of this class.

Wrong political ideology and development policies

The developing world is experiencing a revolution unlike any other it has ever known. No strangers to tumult, countries in Latin America, Africa, the Middle East and Eastern Europe are for the first time embracing capitalism. Their success or failure will depend in a large part on whether they can make the transition from the old world of comparative advantage – relying on abundant natural resources, sunshine and cheap labour – to the new world of competitive advantage: making strategic choices in an age of global markets and networked organisations (Fairbanks & Lindsay, 1997).

Bates (1981) has argued that African politicians chose policies that served their own interests rather than those that favoured national economic development. Therefore, countries did not adopt policies that favoured national strategies for growth and development; instead, leaders adopted policies, strategies and frameworks that ensured their personal benefit. Such a self-serving pattern of politics after independence was bad for development.

The second approach was the adoption of socialism. President Nyerere, who promoted Ujamaa, a form of socialism adopted in Tanzania, said that the African societies of the times, without a class of professionals or a middle class to steer the private sector, were suited to socialism. By nature, Africans were themselves socialist, with communal ownership of productive assets, such as land. At independence, with agrarian economies and support from the USSR, most African states adopted a socialistic or dual economy. The strong belief in the role of the state as the manager of national resources was adopted as the new approach by African independent states. Most revolutionaries, including Nelson Mandela, were perceived by the West as communists or socialists.[10]

As we have come to know, communism or socialism failed to deliver growth and welfare in African societies. And as Keynes

104

wrote: ' . . . Communism is discredited by events; socialism, in its old-fashioned interpretation, no longer interests the world' (Skidelsky, 1992: 121). The belief in communal ownership discouraged competitiveness and self-interest. Governments saw themselves as sole national providers of the needs of society, and in Africa, this failed to solve problems associated with poverty. Begging for aid continued. It is only recently that most African countries have accepted a private-sector orientation in national development. The only problem has been that, after accepting economic liberalisation, leaders forget the vital roles played by the state in regulating, influencing and facilitating the economic sector. The global financial crisis and comments from world leaders, such as former UK Prime Minister Gordon Brown, that the financial sector has become greedy, have left people wondering whether 'capitalism has lost its self-confidence', as Keynes noted (Skidelsky, 1992: 121).

Aid to Africa is not working

Since independence, Africa has received plenty of aid for development, but it is still one of the poorest continents on the earth. Using Dambisa Moyo's[11] definition of foreign aid, we will refer to aid as the total sum of both concessional loans and grants. This definition refers only to official development assistance.

For Africa, aid is not working, yet donors continue to give it. Since 1970, Africa has received at least $300 billion. But the continent is still poor. Many reasons have been put forward to account for the continent's poor growth. They include its geography, history, the large diversity of ethnic groups and lack of strong institutions. These reasons cannot be denied. For example, the history of colonialism influenced Africa's population numbers and the continent's growth and development path, as explained earlier.

In terms of geography, many landlocked countries on the continent have suffered as a result of lack of access to cheap means of transport. It is difficult and expensive for landlocked countries, such as Burundi, Rwanda, Swaziland, Zambia and Uganda, to transport goods by sea. Swaziland and Burundi have only one small airport. Burundi's export and import merchandise has to pass through Kenya, Uganda and Rwanda via Mombasa, a journey of more than 2 000 kilometres on poor roads.

Cultural factors and ethnicity have meant continued border clashes and conflicts. It has not been only conflicts and war in Rwanda that have accounted for its slow growth in the past. Most land in Rwanda is mountainous and unsuitable for farming. Yet these factors do not tell the whole story. Switzerland, also land-locked and mountainous, is developed and prosperous. Saudi Arabia has a desert climate, but has managed to realise high and sustained levels of growth, and it is an advanced developing country. Most people attribute this to oil. But the DRC also has oil and other reserves – yet it still has high rates of poverty. Therefore, the question to ask is, with development assistance or aid accounting for about 15 per cent of its GDP, why has Africa failed to transform itself into an economic giant?

Developed countries in Western Europe, even after the ravages of war, were not dependent on aid. The level of aid to these countries was relatively small and the duration short. Most of these countries received less than 10 per cent of their national income or GDP, mainly from the US under the Marshall Plan. Few countries in Africa have graduated from receiving aid from the World Bank's International Development Assistance (IDA). Worldwide, 22 countries have stopped taking aid from IDA and they are among the most economically successful emerging economies of the 1990s and 2000s. Of these countries, only four, however, are in Africa: Botswana, Equatorial Guinea (after the discovery of oil there), Swaziland and Mauritius. Some of the successful economies outside Africa have a spirit of hard work and good morale; they have efficient public trade promotion agencies and strong legal systems. These factors encourage private-sector development and competitiveness. Most African sub-Saharan countries have been recipients of development assistance accounting for more than 10 per cent of their budgets. For instance, until 2007, Uganda received more than 45 per cent of its budget from aid. It now receives more than 20 per cent. This is progress, but not enough. Even 3 per cent of aid constitutes a large portion of a country's budget.

There have been arguments that Kenya, for example, has for the last five years or so been able to provide 97 per cent of its total fiscal budget, so why not live within its own means and control expenditure? The government could cut the fleet of vehicles given to ministers and other top civil servants, for example.[12] Aid is attractive to leaders and technocrats. It is easy to steal and 'account for'. Public servants can 'cook the books' and show that money was spent according to plans and without waste. Even the budgetary needs to be covered by aid can be inflated. During the procurement process, public officers may agree with the supplier that a 10 per cent kickback be built into the pricing structure, to be shared at a later date.

One way to understand this is to compare the prices for private-sector purchases with government prices. Governments often procure items at prices that are double or even triple the market price.

A negative effect of aid is that it breeds the desire to continue borrowing. And often borrowing is associated with lack of independence by a country when it comes to decision making. Policies are often forced on the borrowers under conditionality.

With the exception of disasters, when relief agencies step in to help, African countries should not wait for food aid. The solution to sustaining rapid population growth is not by attracting more aid. It is through increased production and attracting foreign direct investment (FDI). It is through exchanging goods and services across borders. Trade is the solution. Aid is temporary relief. The need for an aid exit strategy is urgent.

Attracting more foreign direct investment

From the 1970s until 1997, the amount of FDI to Africa was meagre. Instead, there was more aid in the form of grants and conditional loans. The situation has changed and there is now more FDI coming to Africa, although some investors remain sceptical about the political risks, security, peace and unclear economic policies of some African countries. They fear nationalisation and that their business investments will be given away by unscrupulous politicians. And they are not far from reality. This happened in Uganda in the 1970s and more recently in Zimbabwe. However, there seems to be renewed interest in FDI in Africa. In the sub-Saharan region, net private capital inflows increased from $35.8 billion in 2009 to an estimated $41.1 billion in 2010 and were projected to rise to $48.6 billion in 2011 (World Bank, 2011).

There are two schools of thought on the role played by FDI on economic growth, employment and poverty reduction in the developing countries of Africa. There is the argument that FDIs do not create meaningful employment, and thereby income to the locals, because most jobs are taken by foreigners who come with the investor's entourage. This is a problem of government failing to enforce its laws to regulate immigration and employment. But some countries, Tanzania being an example, have decided to address this situation by ensuring that genuine investors are protected.[13] Those investors who are known for the abuse of immigration and labour laws are punished, and this may include deportation. However, there are real benefits to be had from FDI. Through joint ventures involving both domestic and foreign investors, African countries have entered into businesses hitherto not engaged in. For example, countries such as Zambia, Uganda,

Kenya and Rwanda – traditionally mining and agricultural producers – now also export flowers, mainly to the EU and Japan.

Public-private partnerships

The private sector has plenty of money to help fund projects. The government has the capacity to mobilise money and other resources. Countries that focus on serving the market in order to enhance economic growth require infrastructure – roads, ports, harbours, airports, warehousing, railways, etc. Partnership between government and the private sector can ensure that such infrastructure is established. These projects require a lot of financial resources that can neither be provided by an individual investor nor government, and they are long term, so public-private partnership (PPP) is necessary to ensure that such projects are completed. There are still challenges for government in terms of understanding and implementing such partnerships. For example, government may face challenges of costing the items required for such a partnership. Businesspeople may over-cost items and government ultimately ends up putting in more than the private investor without comprehending it. The other issue with PPP is that well-connected private-sector entities are the ones who win the PPP contracts, even when they may not be the most qualified or capable.

Remittances as a form of capital for economic growth

Instead of turning to the Western powers with cap in hand, African governments would be better advised to talk to their expatriates overseas and convince them to invest back home. Some of them have the capital and technological know-how required at home. They need to be assured of the existence of an enabling business environment. China has successfully persuaded the Chinese diaspora to invest back home in China. African countries should start promotion campaigns and offer attractive incentives to encourage the African diaspora to invest in their home countries.

A joint report and fact sheet, *Leveraging Migration for Africa* (World Bank & African Development Bank, 2011) has interesting findings. The report reveals that remittances (i.e. money sent home by diasporic Africans) have become Africa's largest source of net foreign inflows after FDI. Among the findings of this report, in 2010, the continent's remittances were $40 billion, or 2.6 per cent of the continent's total GDP. Sub-Saharan Africa received half of this total. However, the actual figure for the region may be more because of a lack of data on remittances in most countries in the region. Some countries have no data available on remittances.[14] These remittances have come from about 30 million Africans[15] (about 3 per cent of the continent's total population), who have migrated internationally, either voluntarily or as refugees. Available figures show that remittance flows to the continent are similar in size to official aid flows. They accounted for two-thirds of official aid to sub-Saharan Africa (2.2 per cent of GDP versus 3.7 per cent of GDP) in 2010. It is significant to mention that Nigeria alone received $10 billion, almost half of all officially recorded remittances to sub-Saharan Africa in 2010. And in terms of share of GDP, the largest recipient was Lesotho (28.5 per cent), followed by Togo (10.7 per cent), Cape Verde (9.4 per cent), Senegal (9.3 per cent) and The Gambia (8.2 per cent).

As a share of total investment, remittances represented 36 per cent in Burkina Faso, 55 per cent in Kenya, 57 per cent in Nigeria, 15 per cent in Senegal and 20 per cent in Uganda. These funds have contributed significantly in some sub-Saharan African countries. Migrant remittances can help contribute to a country's international reserves, finance imports and improve the current account position[16] of recipient countries. Remittances to sub-Saharan African countries were mostly invested in land, fixed property and starting a business. Some of it was also used to pay school fees for siblings and other relatives.

Clearly, remittances are important for poverty reduction, wealth creation, investment and economic growth. But what have the sub-Saharan countries done to ensure that there is a system that allows the smooth flow of remittances into their economies? This is important. Surveys have shown that only a few countries in the region have established such systems. Ghana, Nigeria and Senegal have developed plans to incorporate diaspora communities as partners in development programmes. This has to be done in all countries so that the diaspora can remit more to their home countries. Experience in some countries reveals that without a formal banking system that allows the flow of remittances, most of it ends up in the hands of criminals and those who do not honour the agreements for the money's intended purpose.[17] Governments will have to implement measures to ensure that mobile money, a quick and cheap way of sending money to people without a bank account or a bank near them, is monitored, as is done with the banking system. This is for the purposes of protecting mainly the sender and the economy from dirty money. Otherwise it is an innovative way of having 'wall-less' banks.

Stopping capital flight

Capital flight occurs in several ways. This book will focus on two: money earnt through corruption and banked in Europe and the US, and total repatriation of investors' earnings to home countries or their accounts in Europe or the US. Although anti-terrorism and anti-money-laundering laws enacted in the US and UK (and other powerful countries) have lessened the flow of capital from Africa, it has not fully stopped it. And not all countries in Africa have enacted such laws. Where they have been enacted, the money that was hitherto stolen and banked abroad by corrupt government officials manifests itself instead in other forms. It is invested locally and mainly in property. For example, recently Kampala has had several new high-rise buildings, mainly shopping malls. We cannot point to which may have been built using corrupt money; we can only allude to it. Although they are a naive form of investment, these buildings are worth millions of dollars. And as people continue to wonder about the source of this money, the fact remains that the construction is happening in Africa.

African countries, therefore, need to revise their investment codes to ensure that investors do not take out of the country all of their earnings.[18] This will create more locally generated financial resources for further investment. The current investment laws were enacted under pressure from donors and multilateral lending agencies. The reasons given were that African countries possessed high political and economic risks. While these risks do remain, they have diminished. Today there are more countries that are no longer under conflict and respect the rule of law. And the socialist ideologies that were adopted at independence have completely waned. All African states have embraced the liberalised market economy. Most of these economies have adopted a private-sector-led approach to directing economic growth. Such countries need to embark on fair play in the private sector, with laws that enhance competitiveness and stimulate economic growth while generating employment.

Central banks and interest rates

The central banks have power and influence over the banking sector in the emerging countries of Africa (and indeed in developed countries). While the central bank cannot fix the rates at which commercial banks lend to their customers, it has several ways of reducing these rates. First, the central bank can reduce the rate at which it lends to the commercial banks. The central bank is a lender of last resort. This gives it leverage over lending in a country. The central bank is a key player in stimulating economic growth. Working with the ministries of finance and planning, it is responsible for good monetary policy to control inflation and ensure that the exchange rate regime is flexible. In most African countries, it implements the banking act or laws. It has the responsibility of setting the levels of capital or liquidity for commercial banks. It also licences commercial banks and other financial organisations. So it has a clear mandate over the performance of the banking sector. It can, therefore, use this position to urge commercial banks to reduce interest rates. It can also advise government on how to set up development banks that have better lending rates. Although sometimes opposed by multilateral lenders, the central bank can also establish a credit guarantee scheme and an export refinance scheme[19] to help boost key strategic sectors and investment. An export financing scheme is subject to lower rates of interest so investors find it attractive. It also has a political function in facilitating government's endeavour to grow the private sector.

Credit reference bureaus

A credit reference bureau (CRB) is an important agency. It reduces banks' concerns over customers' ability to repay loans, and hence contributes to reducing commercial interest rates. A CRB collects information about potential and actual bank customers and uses it to advise (at a fee) banks about actual and potential borrowers: whether to trust and lend to certain clients. It is a function of the central bank to establish such organisations. Individuals' credit history and credit worthiness are available through the CRB. This provides information to financial institutions about a customer's likelihood of defaulting on a financial loan. Reducing the rate of loan repayments should reduce the commercial banks' lending interest rates. This has two key positive outcomes. First, the banks will attract more customers looking for loans, attracted by lower interest rates. Second, the borrowers will invest more and help the government to get more tax revenue and exports. This will enhance national growth and employment-creation efforts.

Microfinance

What has been agreed upon by scholars, the developed world and African leaders themselves is that Africa does not lack resources. Instead, what is lacking is the management of these resources and mobilisation of financial resources to turn natural resources and human capital into marketable items in global trade. Most small and medium-sized enterprises lack requirements for commercial bank loans. They often have no acceptable collateral security. And because of low levels of financial literacy, most people do not understand banking. People in African countries prefer to keep their money at home.

Microfinance is another source of credit, especially for small businesses. In Africa microfinance has a long history, which was initially organised in an informal setting. Small groups organised along village, clan or family lines; people would organise funds to lend to its members. These are never registered by government. In recent times, especially since the start of the new millennium, the microfinance industry has been growing, and is playing a vital role as a financial tool in boosting economic growth. Governments have facilitated the establishment of formal microfinance institutions (commonly known as MFIs). Countries in sub-Saharan Africa, including Mozambique, Ghana, Gabon and Uganda, have seen high levels of growth in the MFI sector in rural and urban areas alike. MFIs have become popular in this region, as many people and businesses do not have valuable assets as security for a loan, they do not require large loans (which the banks are interested in selling) or they do not have saving accounts to support their loan application.

It was the view of Nobel Laureate Muhammad Yunus, founder of Grameen Bank, that it is the rich who can borrow from traditional banks, but that the poor people cannot because of these banks' stringent requirements (Shinn, 2009). To be able to borrow, therefore, requires that they form small groups. These groups can then form small businesses or associations and go to an MFI for a loan. They may not necessarily be subject to the stringent demands applied by traditional banks. However, MFIs charge higher rates than traditional commercial banks. Microfinance lending rates are higher than commercial banking rates on an annual basis. The high rates are associated, among other factors, with the risk of borrowers' failure to repay and the cost of reaching borrowers.[20] However, because MFIs require less collateral than commercial banks, small borrowers often accept the terms without choice. The role of government then is to work with the central bank to ensure that interest rates are not high. Rather than attempt to control commercial lending rates by dictating the rates, government through the central bank can facilitate transparent pricing in commercial banks and microfinance products.

This can be done by the central banks as the licensor of these institutions in most countries. Engaging in constructive dialogue with macrofinance support centres or overseers and the key microfinance organisations can open up new potential for small businesses in Africa.

Borrowers may pay lower interest if there is an initiative to impel MFIs to price loans fairly. This also necessitates education programmes to make citizens aware of interest rates. Such programmes will make small borrowers aware of the pricing of products and other key information. Such information will also reduce the fear of borrowing, thereby increasing the number of borrowers in the economy. And this translates into growth by increasing the number of small businesses, and would propel African economies in ways that have never been seen before.

Despite the high charges associated with microfinance loans, these institutions are still important for the growth equation of sub-Saharan economies. They should, therefore, be encouraged by government, as they are an alternative source of funds for small local investors. Governments – and in particular the central banks – in the region should monitor and regulate any possible overcharges through dialogue and advice to the microfinance sector.

The securities exchange and stock exchange

Some individuals and companies keep their money in the bank. It can only be accessed by themselves, which is counterproductive. This money should be invested in stocks. In this way, the money circulates, changes hands and creates more investors, especially small investors who would otherwise not be able to afford to buy a company on their own. This has the advantage of pooling resources to the formal banking sector directly.

Securities exchange has been viewed positively by most governments in the region. And this is a good step towards a domestic capital solution to these economies. The growth in stock exchanges is impressive. Two decades ago, there were only five stock exchanges in sub-Saharan Africa. Today the region has more than 20. The region also has one regional stock exchange domiciled in Abidjan, currently serving the francophone[21] countries of West Africa. The East African Community is in the process of establishing a regional stock exchange to consolidate its thinly capitalised country stock markets. Similar efforts are being undertaken in southern Africa under SADC.

The rapid growth in the number of stock exchanges in the region has been attributed to the extensive financial-sector reforms undertaken by African countries during the economic liberalisation and privatisation of state-owned commercial banks. These reforms included various measures, such as interest rate liberalisation, liberalisation of foreign-exchange markets, removal of credit ceilings, privatisation of state-owned commercial banks – and improved government supervision and regulation, promotion and development of capital markets – which included the establishment of money and stock markets. These markets are still small and facing illiquidity. There is, therefore, a need for government to continue urging companies to list on the stock exchange. With the exception of South Africa, the sub-Saharan markets are the smallest of any region in the world in terms of the number of companies listed on the stock exchange and market capitalisation.[22] Some of the exchanges still do not operate daily. Business will increase once investors know that they are always open, and governments ought to be thinking in this direction.

Financial literacy campaigns

In the same way that most governments in Africa have invested in campaigns to raise awareness of HIV/AIDS, now is the time to begin aggressive campaigns at political rallies, in the media, in churches, mosques and other places of worship promoting financial literacy.[23] People need to understand the benefits of producing and selling to the market. They also need to understand the importance of money and saving. They need to understand how banks are used both for saving and obtaining credit. This puts money in the banking sector, which can be lent out. Governments in sub-Saharan Africa have to start on financial enlightenment as a key approach to promoting increased banking and investment by the common people in their economies. When money is 'kept under the bed' and not put in the formal banking sector, there is a problem for the economy: the economy may lack the required finance to lend and use in investment in key sectors. This makes economies resort to external sources of funds, including aid.

There is also a need to encourage a cultural shift in thinking in terms of eating most of the produce and selling only the surplus. Financial literacy encourages people not only to bank, but also the importance of the market – and market operations, as opposed to living according to a subsistence economy. Money has to be viewed as the 'best vitamin' in the world, to use the words of a young boy to this author's former classmate.

Property rights and land titles

Property rights, especially ownership and land rights, are important for individuals and help families mobilise resources for investment by using title as collateral security in financial institutions.

Earlier ideological differences on private property existed between the Marxists and free-market proponents. While the Marxists said that private property was theft, the free-market thinkers, such as economics Nobel Laureate Milton Friedman, put it that private property was central to freedom. In Friedman's words:

> If you don't control your property, if somebody else controls it, they're going to decide what to do with it, and you have no possibility of exercising influence on it . . . Nobody spends somebody else's money as carefully as he spends his own. Nobody uses somebody else's resources as carefully as he uses his own. So if you want efficiency and effectiveness, if you want knowledge to be properly utilized, you have to do it through the means of private property.[24]

More recently, Peruvian development economist Hernando de Soto in his book *The Mystery of Capital* emphasised the importance of people's rights to what they own. In most African countries many people have capital without rights to it. De Soto calls this 'dead capital'. They own land, but have no land title. So they cannot get loans from the banks because they have no collateral security. They may have been using this land for hundreds of years and no one else claims it, but they cannot transfer ownership except to their relatives. This is one other structural problem that governments ought to attend to. Governments in Africa should help the citizens and permanent residents to acquire titles for their properties, especially land and their houses. In the developed world, owners claim title to their property; it can be valued and a figure attached to it. The titles can be used to negotiate loans from banks or as share capital in a joint investment.

Land is the most important asset for wealth creation in most African countries, especially given that most people in rural areas depend on agriculture. According to a UN Fund for Agriculture paper, the arguments in favour of registering title to land most commonly used are:

- Land registration stimulates a more efficient use of the land because it increases tenure security and removes disincentives to invest in the longer-term management and productivity of the land.
- Land registration enables the creation of a land market, allowing land to be transferred from less to more dynamic farmers and consolidated into larger holdings.
- Land registration provides farmers with a title that can be offered as collateral to financial institutions, thereby improving farmers' access to credit and allowing them to invest in land improvements.
- It provides governments with information regarding landholders and size of fields, which can provide the basis for a system of property taxes (FAO, 2004).

There are, however, problems created by the land tenure systems in the region. In South Sudan, Tanzania, Kenya and Uganda, for example, there are large expanses of land used by communities without any of the persons having title rights to such land. In Kenya and Tanzania, the Masai people (who are herdsmen) have been living on large tracts of land practising transhumant nomadism (characterised by seasonal migration) for ages, but none of them can claim ownership to that land. It is just referred to as Masai land. In northern Uganda, those who are not cattle keepers but farmers also live on land that is communally owned. This system of land ownership has caused conflicts in northern Ghana, bitter civil war in the Ivory Coast, Burundi, Rwanda, the DRC, and even among communities in southern Africa (including South Africa). This land tenure system, referred to as customary or communal land ownership, does not allow individuals to have rights on land. The community cannot allow one individual to lease parts of it. It can only be used by the same ethnic group. They can only leave (especially at death) the part they have been living and growing food on to their children. This is the only form of transfer allowed.

In some other countries, people have failed to develop land because of absentee landlords. Individuals who own land often inherited it from chiefs and other African rulers before colonialism. Their fathers were given this land when they acted as collaborators and helped extend the colonial empire to other ethnic groups. This land belonged to the inhabitants of the area that these African chiefs helped the colonialist to subdue. So they took the land and titled it when the actual owners were on the land. Much later they are told that they are not the lawful owners of the land. If this land were to be sold off to other people, it would help increase the population's access to and investment in this land. It would increase production and stimulate economic growth. The biggest problem with the region is that they view their assets in terms of buildings, animals and vehicles, but do not treat land as an asset.

Government has to help people with regard to land rights. A person who has long used a certain piece of land, and where there are no conflictual claims over it, should be entitled to legal ownership of that land. This title is important for the legal transfer of property, rents and collateral to obtain loans from banks.

Regional and international trade relations

Intra-African economic cooperation

Given that markets in sub-Saharan Africa are small in terms of purchasing power parity, there is a need for these economies to form a regional bloc to enhance economic cooperation and trade. Regional integration has several benefits for the member states. There is the advantage of becoming a big internal market. For instance, the Economic Community of West African States (ECOWAS)[1] has a total population of 252 million, and the East African Community (EAC) around 131 million. Disparate states that lack individual economic power can, therefore, gain collectively from being part of a big market. A manufacturer of maize meal, for example, can sell it anywhere in the region, and will benefit from paying local taxes.

There is another important benefit of such blocs. They lessen border conflicts between these countries. Whenever such conflicts arise, it is easier to handle them at a regional level. In the EAC region, for example, conflict over ownership of the tiny island of Migingo in Lake Victoria between Kenya and Uganda is being handled at the EAC regional level. If these countries were not able to cooperate under the EAC, this conflict had the potential to escalate into a serious regional conflict.

Further integration into a full monetary area (or union) has the benefit of a single currency and standardised monetary policy.

(Caution must be taken to ensure that all member states adhere to the principles and rules to avoid the challenges facing the EU under the Eurozone.) The single currency reduces the disadvantages of currency exchange and convertibility. Traders from other countries find it easier to trade with an economic bloc. One can also sum the importance of regional integration using the business adage that 'the customer is the king'. Because countries come together to trade, they are held by the need to make money from the relationship. They cannot fight their neighbours, who are their customers – their 'kings'.

At a higher level, countries can form themselves into one political federation with a regional government and a parliament. The European Union (EU) is a good example of a regional integration that has been beneficial to its people.[2] It has a regional government, a parliament and a monetary union (and the EU Central Bank). While individual countries can have bilateral relations with other countries, the European Commission (EC) enters into bilateral relations with other customs unions and countries on behalf of all the EU membership. While each country may have its own views on the World Trade Organisation (WTO) agreements and negotiations (for example, France has strong views on farming as a way of life), it is the EC that ultimately enters into agreements under the WTO. We ought to be reminded, too, that the US is a confederation of several different states.

Returning to sub-Saharan Africa, if one considers the EAC, one finds that the communities at the borders share a similar culture (this is the same in other blocs, like ECOWAS). Under regional integration, the Banyarwanda people of Uganda, Tanzania and those of Rwanda can freely interact without visas. The Samia of Kenya and those of Uganda can also visit and work in either country without the restrictions of visas and permits.

Despite the benefits of regional economic blocs, it is a priority, however, for the African Union to reduce the number of regional economic communities (RECs) and the overlaps in order to achieve meaningful development. The large number of RECs (some of which are small in market size) leads to costly competition for resources, fragmentation of markets and restriction in the growth potential of regions, unnecessary duplication of functions and bureaucracy, conflict and inconsistencies in the formulation and implementation of policies on tax, movement of labour and services.

Ideally, a country should belong to just one REC. This will help to avoid the conflicts created by the issues of taxing commodities moving from one REC to another, where some members belong to both and others to one. Each REC as a common market or customs union has its own common external tariff (CET). The table shows that some countries belong to more than one REC.

Regional economic communities and their member states

REGIONAL ECONOMIC COMMUNITIES[3] (RECs)	COUNTRIES
ECOWAS Economic Community of West African States	Benin, Burkina Faso, Cape Verde, Côte d'Ivoire, The Gambia, Ghana, Guinea, Guinea-Bissau, Liberia, Mali, Nigeria, Niger, Senegal, Sierra Leone, Togo
COMESA Common Market for Eastern and Southern Africa	Burundi, Comoros, Congo, DRC, Djibouti, Egypt, Eritrea, Ethiopia, Kenya, Libya, Madagascar, Malawi, Mauritius, Rwanda, Seychelles, Sudan, Swaziland, Uganda, Zambia, Zimbabwe, South Sudan
SADC Southern Africa Development Community	Angola, Botswana, DRC, Lesotho, Madagascar, Malawi, Mauritius, Mozambique, Namibia, Seychelles, South Africa, Swaziland, Tanzania, Zambia, Zimbabwe
EAC East African Community	Kenya, Uganda, Tanzania, Rwanda, Burundi

REGIONAL ECONOMIC COMMUNITIES (RECs)	COUNTRIES
IGAD Inter-Governmental Authority on Development	Djibouti, Eritrea, Ethiopia, Kenya, Somalia, Sudan, Uganda
CEN SAD Community of Sahel-Saharan States	Burkina Faso, Chad, Libya, Mali, Niger, Sudan, Central African Republic, Eritrea, Djibouti, Gambia, Senegal, Egypt, Morocco, Nigeria, Somalia, Tunisia, Benin, Togo, Côte d'Ivoire, Guinea-Bissau, Liberia, Ghana, Sierra Leone, Comoros, Guinea
ECCAS Economic Community of Central African States	Burundi, Cameroon, Central African Republic, Chad, Congo, DRC, Equatorial Guinea, Gabon, São Tomé and Príncipe, Angola
AMU Arab Magreb Union	Algeria, Libya, Mauritania, Morocco, Tunisia
CEMAC Economic and Monetary Community of Central Africa	Cameroon, Central African Republic, Chad, Republic of Congo, Guinea, Gabon
UEMOA *Union Economique et Monetaire Ouest Africaine*	Benin, Burkina Faso, Côte d'Ivoire, Mali, Niger, Senegal, Togo
SACU Southern African Customs Union	Namibia, Swaziland, Botswana, Lesotho, South Africa

Source: Author's compilation using REC websites and national government sources

While efforts continue at forming a continent-wide African union, for now regional blocs must suffice. They will help build regional capacities and markets. In the long run, however, there is a need for an Africa-wide organisation that will critically address mainly economic and political issues facing the continent. This will not only address the challenges of the sub-Saharan region, but also emerging political issues in Arab Africa. This organisation will be needed in order to give Africans power to debate and address African issues in Africa. The unending claims, for example, that the continent is being 'recolonised' by Europe, supported by the US, will be addressed by such a pan-African organisation. If problems cannot be solved at the continental level, then one would have to turn to the UN.

A new partnership with Africa: Trade, not aid

The EU and African countries have had formal trade and development relations since 1975, when the members of the then European Community and the African, Caribbean and Pacific Group of States (ACP) signed a trade agreement (Lomé 1) in Lomé, Togo. By 2000, these partners had signed up to five Lomé conventions, under which the ACP states had been given both duty-free and quota-free market access to the EU market, on a non-reciprocal arrangement. The ACP countries did not (and they didn't have to) remove all the tariffs on imports from the EU.

When these conventions expired, the partners signed yet another partnership agreement, the Cotonou Partnership Agreement (CPA). After negotiations, the CPA was concluded on 23 June 2000 in Cotonou, Benin, to be in force for 20 years. It contains a clause allowing it to be revised every five years. In the same agreement, the partners agreed to negotiate a reciprocal trade and development arrangement, referred to as the Economic Partnership Agreements (commonly known by its abbreviation – EPA).

Did the ACP countries manage to increase the volume and quality of exports to the EU during the period of free market access (the non-reciprocal arrangement)? The answer is no. The problems were both domestic to African countries and external – that is, in the EU markets. In Africa there was not enough production and the quality of exports to the EU was poor. In the EU, trade barriers, such as certification and stringent standards, remained an obstacle. What types of African exports have entered Europe since 1975? Mainly primary-sector goods (raw materials) and agricultural products, in other words, unprocessed products that often fetch little for African economies. There is, therefore, a need for a meaningful partnership between the two regions to help boost African value-added trade. If the EU wants products from Africa, they need to work with countries in Africa to access these products and improve the quality. The Chinese offer some good lessons for partnership in trade. The Chinese have built infra-structure to access the sources of the raw materials they want from Africa. We will look at this later in the chapter.

New US-Africa trade relations

During the period of the Cold War, the US and the USSR tried to win converts to their ideologies. Africa was caught in the middle, pulled to one side or the other by foreign aid. The superpowers often supported wrong leaders, such as Mobutu of Zaire (DRC) and Idi Amin of Uganda. Charles Taylor of Liberia cooperated with CIA agents, originally to spy on Gaddaffi.[4] Hopefully that era is now gone.

In 2003, the US granted some countries in the sub-Saharan region the African Growth and Opportunities Act (AGOA).[5] There are about 40 countries[6] that benefit from this trade preferences entry scheme. These trade preferences were established after President Clinton issued a proclamation in October 2000 by first designating 34 countries in sub-Saharan Africa as eligible for the trade benefits of the AGOA. In most cases, the AGOA has not been a success. Some of the reasons for this failing have been internal to the countries supposed to benefit under the AGOA. There were problems of quantity and quality, and most of these countries were not well prepared by their governments to benefit from it. Mauritius, however, which had been waiting for this opportunity, gained from it.[7]

Recently, the US signed a trade and investment agreement with the EAC region, an indication that the US is interested in trading with regions of sub-Saharan Africa. The US market is lucrative if preparations are made well by African countries to enter it. The requirements of democracy, the Western style of trade relations, however, might still pose an obstacle to African countries wishing to penetrate the US market. That is why China may offer better opportunities for trade with Africa. It is a very large market and, being a developing country, its standards and quality requirements are likely to be met by sub-Saharan exporters.

The influence of Arab countries

The Arab countries are interested in Africa and are looking for business. They have both money and influence in Africa. They have extended aid directly to governments and indirectly to educational and health institutions, among other areas. They are giving scholarships to students to study in Arab countries, to learn the Arab way of life and languages. They have started opening banks in sub-Saharan Africa and soon courses in Islamic banking will commence. They are interested in the same types of products that Africa exports to the EU, and maybe the US. Entry requirements into these markets, though not light, are not as stringent as is the case with the EU and the US. Africa would be well advised to explore this market. Diversified markets, such as in the Arab world, offer Africa an opportunity for export revenue – reducing its 'beggar' syndrome and dependence on aid.

China in Africa: Is China Africa's friend?

China's economic rise is a historical and ongoing process that started in the late 1970s when a reform and open-door policy was adopted. While it remains probably the only surviving socialist republic in the world, it has undertaken reforms aimed at benefiting from markets in different parts of the world. It still uses state enterprises to invest and trade with Africa and other parts of the world, such as Latin America.

China is not in the club of the rich and developed countries; it is not a member of the G8 (UK, US, Canada, Germany, France, Japan, Italy and Russia). Despite its rapid growth, China is still a developing country – although it is probably developing faster than most other developing countries. While it has embraced market economics, unlike the US's capitalist democracy, China wants to consolidate its socialist democracy with its own blend of market socialism. It still has a substantial population living in poor conditions, and the state enterprise does business on behalf of the Chinese people.

China is one of the world's longest-enduring civilisations, with a documented history spanning 4 600 years. With a territorial extension of 9.6 million square kilometres, China is the third-largest country in the world and with nearly a fifth of the world's population, at 1.34 billion.[8] It accounts for around 25 per cent of world trade. It is also the second-largest consumer of oil products in the world, after the US, accounting for 9.4 per cent of world petroleum consumption. Like the other trading partners of Africa, China needs raw materials and markets for its own products.

China's direct investments in Africa were approximately $1.6 billion in 2005. China's trade with Africa is growing. Between 2007 and 2010 figures show an FDI average of about $1.5 billion per year.[9] The FDI into Africa in 2010 was reported to be $2.1 billion, with a stock of FDI at $13 billion.[10] According to the Chinese Ministry of Commerce, total trade between China and Africa (North Africa included) was expected to reach $110 billion in 2010.[11] It increased from $9.5 billion in 2000 to $36.3 billion in 2005, and then to $79.8 billion in 2009 (Cheung, De Haan & Yu, 2011).

As indicated by China's imports from Africa, it is clear where its main interests lie: fuel and mineral resources. From an analysis based on the World Trade Organisation Data Statistics online for 2004 to 2008, 87 per cent of China's imports from Africa are fuels and minerals. As with the EU, China has developed a strategy for Africa, the China Africa Strategy. It has also established a forum with African leaders.[12]

In particular, the Chinese import oil and other raw materials from South Sudan, Uganda, DRC, Angola and several other countries. To reach areas where oil and other minerals are extracted requires good roads and other infrastructure, which the Chinese are providing. Good infrastructure is also good for access to markets for other African commodities. The Chinese have built bridges in the DRC, roads in Uganda, railways in Angola, mass rail transit systems in Nigeria, power stations in Zambia and high-voltage power transmission lines to interconnect countries in southern Africa. Chinese-funded ICT projects include the roll-out of a national communications network in Ethiopia and the construction of new lines linked to mining projects in Gabon and Mauritania (Schiere & Rugamba, 2011). According to the African Development Bank, China's investment in African infrastructure remained stable, at around $5 billion per year in the period 2005–2009; the bank says that such investment activities totalled at $15.9 billion in 2010.

There have been allegations that China has been supplying arms to countries experiencing internal problems, for example, in Darfur, Sudan.[13] This is not good for trade, which does not thrive during conflict. So critics think that China's entry into Africa with investments, trade and aid is likely to worsen Africa's pace towards democratisation and observance of human rights. Zimbabwe was able to buy a military aircraft from China after the West had put an embargo on Mugabe. And China has invested in Zimbabwe, which is currently boycotted by investors from developed countries. There are also allegations of fake and counterfeit Chinese goods exported to Africa. Therefore, Chinese interests in the region are not without their challenges.

India in Africa

India is another significant trade partner in the region. India has achieved sustained levels of growth driven by industrialisation, trade and information technology. It has a big domestic market. The same market can become a market for African products. Like China, India's manufactured products are all over Africa. Some of these have quality issues. Indians have invested in Africa, despite unsubstantiated claims of being just managers or stooges of the investments they claim to own. The claims are that African corrupt leaders provide the cash while the Indians run the businesses. It is difficult to substantiate such claims. This, however, does not negate the fact that there are genuine Indian investors helping African economies by creating jobs, helping stakeholders earn revenue and paying taxes. And more of them are needed. In fact, what is relevant is not the origin of the investor but the benefits derived out of the investment: employment, income, tax revenue and enhancing economic growth.

Concluding remarks on the new partnership with Africa

Africa needs new partnership for trade and development from other regions, both developing and developed. The original historical relationships, such as EU-ACP trade and development arrangements, have not been able to deliver more growth (and sustainable revenues from exports) for sub-Saharan Africa. Perhaps this is due to the historical perspective, namely that the EU saw African countries as former colonies that needed to be supported with aid. A close examination of the effect of aid, however, reveals that it cannot develop any country. The more a country receives aid, the worse its economic position becomes. From 1980 to the 2000s, the markets of the EU remained largely available for Africa's exports of raw materials and non-processed merchandise, and this has not changed the fortunes of most African countries. Africa needs to engage in meaningful trade. It needs trade partnerships that focus on enhancing Africa's competitiveness, productivity and growth. While there are genuine concerns about democracy and human rights in the less developed and developing countries, this should not stand in the way of meaningful trade. Along the development path there are bound to be ups and downs: democracy may falter and human rights may suffer, but eventually continued growth will lead to development. Even the developed countries went through these steps historically, with racial discrimination and disenfranchisement of women, but these are now things of the past. Development eliminates human rights abuses and promotes democracy.

And concerns about democracy and human rights have not stopped China-US trade flows. So they should not stop African countries from trading with China, or any other country that is ready to do business. Africa requires different relationships from various countries. Developed countries have markets that Africa needs to be able to access. These countries also have global influence and military might. Countries such as the US control the World Bank and the IMF. They have much influence in the UN. And these countries are important to Africa; they need to open their lucrative markets wider.

All the Western developed countries and advanced countries from the global south are scrambling for Africa's abundant raw materials.[14] Therefore, African countries need partners to utilise its mineral wealth. But caution has to be taken in order for Africa to benefit from those who want raw materials. Initially, Africa can export primary materials at the earlier levels of processing. But with market experience, African countries in the long run should look to enjoy export proceeds of processed mineral goods, which have greater value. The trajectory to development is not an easy or rapid journey, but there should be no opt out.

The global war on terrorism and money laundering requires the cooperation of all regions of the world, including Africa. Africans themselves must take the lead in the fight against terrorism[15] within their continent. Africans best understand the political landscape of the region. They need to exploit the developed countries for what they have most – money and knowledge. Peace and stability are pertinent to economic growth. It is in the interests of the developed world to work towards promoting peace and security in Africa. It does not take a political or military strategist to understand the implications of a big population that is unemployed, poor and divided along the lines of religion and ethnicity.

Access to markets and
'just and fair' trade

Professor Jeffery D. Sachs, advisor to the UN secretary general, in his book *The End of Poverty: How We Can Make it Happen in Our Lifetime*, makes a very important point on the relationship between infrastructure and markets. Sachs says that

> . . . when the preconditions of basic infrastructure (roads, power, and ports) and human capital (health and education) are in place, markets are powerful engines of development. Without those preconditions, markets can cruelly bypass large parts of the world, leaving them impoverished and suffering without respite. Collective action, through effective government provision of health, education, infrastructure, as well as foreign assistance when needed, underpins economic success. (Sachs, 2005: 3)

Governments should provide these preconditions before a free market economy can operate well, and put in place the infrastructure needed to allow the flow of goods and services in local and export markets. Indeed, governments in Africa should only involve themselves in the market system when there is a need for infrastructure, in the case of market failure and to address the imperfections caused by underdeveloped economies. Governments should be cautious about its involvement in the operations of the market in any other way – supply and demand should be left to determine market dynamics. Governments should intervene only to correct market failure, but never to interrupt the working of private-sector processes. The government's major role is to facilitate, influence and regulate the economic activities (Kamugisha, 2011).

Several viewpoints on the importance of trade have been made by civil-society advocates, academia and governments. There is the popular school of thought in the global south that claims that trade between the global north and south has not benefited the poor in the south. Proponents of such a view say trade benefits the rich countries, and that the poor economies are just sources of raw materials for developed countries. There is the second school of thought propounded by those who see trade as good and vital for the economies of developing countries. They argue that trade brings in foreign exchange – and that this money has been earned, not given by donors. This is the viewpoint of the World Bank, the IMF, wealthy countries and government technocrats from developing countries. The intention here is not to discuss schools of thought, but to put forward practical remedies.

Trade enables a country to produce and sell what it does not require or use domestically. Zimbabweans, Kenyans and Ugandans, for example, do not provide a market for flowers. The domestic market for flowers in these countries is very small. However, they produce flowers commercially and export them mainly to the wholesale markets in the Netherlands and Japan. In return, investors, workers and government earn incomes and taxes, respectively. This is trade. It is enhanced by investments – domestic and FDI. You do not have to produce and sell domestically. They may be export markets. To realise more from export receipts, it is necessary to think about quality and quantity. Meaningless and irregular quantities will not yield enough to offset the import bills. Quality and value addition in the supply chain also matter. For example, it is more lucrative to export leather products than unprocessed hides or skins. Value is added to the product in the processing. Similarly, instead of exporting fruit, let government and investors embark on a strategy for the export promotion and development of fruit juice.

There are claims that when added-value products from sub-Saharan Africa are exported to the EU or the US, there are tariff escalations on these products. This is not true, however, for all developing countries exporting to the rich markets.[1] Government's technical specialists on trade issues need to explain these facts to the exporters (and trade advocates who may have some interest in this subject). Because markets are important both at domestic and international levels, governments ought to discourage traditional subsistence production and consumption. Also to be discouraged is selling the surplus to the market. Instead, families should produce for the market first and consume what remains themselves.

Unfair world trade rules: Africa's failure

'The challenge is clear – can we make trade work for all of us; or do we continue with a system with 2 billion locked out of prosperity and denied a chance to work their way out of poverty? This is a test for all of us. A test of our commitment to make globalisation work . . . The benefits of a successful round [the WTO Doha Trade negotiations] are: for the poor – we know a 1 per cent increase in Africa's share of world trade will benefit Africa by over $70 billion, three times the aid increase agreed at Gleneagles [aid promised in 2005 by the G8 – the world's eight most powerful countries].' (Former UK Prime Minister Tony Blair's speech, the *Guardian*, 15 November 2005.)

The main debate on trade policy for economic development usually centres on the questions of how far developing countries should pursue trade liberalisation and how they should open up their economies to foreign trade. There are two polarised schools of thought on trade liberalisation – one for it and the other against it. The liberal trade theorists' school argues for openness and asserts that trade liberalisation enhances growth. The other school is for protectionism. They argue that historically many countries developed by erecting protection barriers (Chang, 2002; 2007).

The literature shows that Singapore is the only country to have made the transition from a least developed country to a developed economy under a wholly liberalised trade regime. Paul Krugman and Maurice Obstfeld (2003) in *International Economics: Theory and Policy* say that Hong Kong is perhaps the only part of the world that genuinely practices free trade. The author has argued in many fora that the US's granting sub-Saharan African countries the African Growth and Opportunity Act (AGOA), a preferential trade arrangement, was a direct admission that the US market was protected. It is not fully open; neither is the EU. The EU gives Africa, and other regions, unilateral and bilateral market preference schemes. The markets of both the rich and advancing countries have high trade barriers.[2]

The less developed countries have continuously alleged foul play and unequal bargaining power, especially at the WTO. These countries have joined other developing countries for trade support. The problem is that they are 'ganging up with' India, Brazil, Argentina and China, countries perceived by the developed countries (and rightly so) as advanced, even though they still have greater numbers of poor than the developed world. So when during negotiations the other parties deny certain benefits to these advanced developing countries, all the African countries suffer. Even the most powerful NGOs with representation in those capitals where key trade and development decisions are made (e.g. Washington, London, Geneva and Brussels) seem to mainly represent the views of India and other advanced developing countries. And some of them have an Indian connection. African NGOs find themselves using India's experience to lobby and advocate for better terms of trade with Africa. What they forget is that India is one of those countries with which Africa should be negotiating for better market entry terms. There is a need for the poor sub-Saharan countries to form a group that can negotiate and lobby for fair and just market access and entry conditions in the global trade arena. This group could eventually form alliances with different groups and countries negotiating at the WTO.

Africa's access to markets is vital

Developed countries provide potential markets for African products. Eventually Africa will develop through trade, good national development policies and good leadership. There are different ways of accessing a market in another country. The country can negotiate with another country or bloc of countries where its businesses want to market their exports. Markets can be accessed via bilateral trade arrangements and membership of a regional trading community, such as SADC. Different African regions are currently negotiating with the EU a free trade arrangement under the ambit of the Cotonou Partnership agreement of 2000, called the Economic Partnership Agreements (commonly known by their acronym – EPA). These negotiations have taken quite some time since early 2000 to date because they are supposedly reciprocal trade arrangements (meaning that both parties have to remove trade barriers, such as import duties, from goods from the EU). The principle of asymmetry is very important here, namely to recognise that developing countries still have economic and political challenges and, therefore, cannot give in equal measure as the EU does. Although the EU should – and is able to – eliminate all tariffs on African imports immediately, the African economies can do so eventually,[3] after a period of time.

A country can also join the WTO and enjoy the benefits of membership under a multilateral trade arrangement. There has been criticism, especially from developing countries, that the WTO is a 'rich man's club'. Nevertheless, it is an important channel for accessing several markets. A country has to weigh the options of not being a member of the WTO – a global trade regulator.

Economic diplomacy

During the time that there were terrorist activities in Northern Ireland, the region was negatively affected. Tourism declined and there were disruptions to transport and normal business operations, for example. Despite this, however, investments continued to trickle into Northern Ireland. The reason is that Northern Ireland was not perceived as a dangerous location by investors. It is the investors who choose where to invest their money. But the positive image of a country is also shaped and moulded by key stakeholders (the media, diplomats, government and the private sector). The government, the private sector and the media had a big role to play in building the name or image of this part of the world, making it an attractive place for investments. But whenever there is a problem in Africa, the international media (and even local media), and diplomats from wealthy countries have not helped much. Indeed, Africa has had its share of dictatorship, maladministration, conflicts and wars. But at times the reports in the media have portrayed these problems as a 'death sentence' and even discouraged trade, investment and tourism into the continent. Of course, no company or individual would wish to invest their money in a war zone. Currently, it may be very risky to invest in African regions such as Somalia, Darfur, Eritrea and eastern DRC, which are experiencing periods of outright conflict. The case of Zimbabwe has already been discussed, which is being boycotted on the basis of such issues as abuse by government.

A fair and balanced reporting is vital for Africa. So it is time for the governments in Africa to start an aggressive marketing or image-building campaign. This does not mean that there are no challenges on the continent. But it is important to explain the current issues and the steps being taken to address them. All countries have experienced challenges at one time or another, but they have been able to communicate and appeal to different stakeholders, mainly the media, the business community, partner countries and their citizens – and have continued to trade. A combination of a country's planned communications and economic diplomacy then helps a great deal. This builds a country's positive image, and whenever the country faces problems, this will be made clear.

The way sub-Saharan countries relate to Europe, the Arab world, the US, Asia and Latin America has to change. The days of being pro-West or pro-East are long gone. Africa should face the future – they should face forward.[4] Capitalism is now the status quo worldwide. Political relations are important but economic relations are paramount. The more the countries relate in economic terms, the better. Was China always a good friend to the US? No, but the two nations do good business together today. This is the real world and African countries need markets, foreign direct investment (FDI), business partners and business agents in foreign markets. During the Cold War and the period immediately afterwards, politics dominated the lives of diplomats. Now that has ended. This is the time for economic diplomacy. Simply put, economic diplomacy means that kind of diplomacy aimed at increasing the level of FDI and reaching a country by attracting more trade.[5] According to Ambassador Tom Amolo, economic diplomacy puts the following considerations together: the use of political influence and relationships to promote trade and investment; improving the functioning of markets; reducing the cost and risk of cross-border transactions; achieving internationally accepted standards; and securing private property rights (investment protection agreements). Kishan Rana, former ambassador of India and professor emeritus at the Foreign Service Institute, India, defines economic diplomacy as the process through which countries tackle the outside world to maximise their national gain in all fields of activity, including trade, investment and other forms of economically beneficial exchanges, where they enjoy comparative advantage (Rana, 2000).

Politics will remain important, too. Western governments will continue to require African countries to make strides towards democratisation and more progress in their observance of human rights. But it is important that these countries obtain markets, attract tourists, get technology to add value and attract FDI through capital, technology and a sound business mentality. African diplomats would be better advised to go to trade meetings with an economic diplomacy agenda and investment proposals instead of attending ceremonious and expensive dinners. Once they have succeeded at economic diplomacy and their countries have achieved sustained growth, then will be the time for celebrating.

Are international NGOs promoting Africa's economic growth?

'In much the same way European empires once dictated policies across their colonial holdings, the new colonialists – among them international development groups, humanitarian non-governmental organizations, faith-based organizations, and megaphilanthropies – direct development strategies and craft government policies for their hosts.'[1]
(*Cohen, Küpçü & Khanna*, 2008[2])

There are several international non-governmental organisations (INGOs)[3] in Africa. Most of them provide relief, emergency and humanitarian assistance, and monitor human rights and governance issues. Their objectives, inter alia, are to help the vulnerable and disadvantaged – and in Africa these are numerous: orphans and widows of war or HIV/AIDS; the poor and the aged without social welfare; those displaced by conflict; victims of drought and epidemics. The list is endless. These organisations have been viewed by the governments of the developed countries as appropriate vehicles for delivering official development assistance. They have been regarded as the necessary 'magic bullet' in fixing the problems that underlie developing countries' development processes.[4] So they have been given financial and other support.[5] Some of them have annual budgets bigger than those of government ministries. In countries such as Tanzania, Burundi or Uganda, certain INGOs have annual budgets in excess of $6 million. Many of these organisations are headed by management teams of foreign experts – in some cases it would appear as if the nationals of such countries do not have the expertise or cannot be trusted.

The work of INGOs tends not to be needs-based (give a farmer tools for farming, for example) but rights-based. This is an approach whereby the NGOs train the people – the poor and the vulnerable – and equip them with the questions to demand their rights. They train them in advocacy. They usually train them in techniques that

143

they can use to rise up and fight or demand their rights. But is it really necessary to organise workshops and training seminars for the poor and vulnerable in luxurious hotels, in locations with PowerPoint facilities? Surely it is more appropriate to train the disadvantaged in their own homes and villages. Is it also enough to train the poor mainly in advocacy (a rights-based approach) without enabling them to work, produce for the market and earn an income? Isn't it the production and marketing of their produce or services that has enhanced the growth and development of developed countries in North America and western Europe? Shouldn't INGOs and their funders be promoting more efforts towards producing for the market and earning income? Isn't there a need for a rethink of how to use both rights-based and needs-based approaches for the greater benefits of the target beneficiaries for poverty eradication, economic growth and democracy?

We know that all is not well with the political leadership in many African states. But it is arguable that INGOs' training in advocacy is not appropriate in terms of removing dictatorships and installing democracy in Africa. Outside the Arab region of Africa, which has its own particular characteristics, the approach so far has not been effective – and these organisations have been here for many decades.

INGOs have been viewed in various ways by African leaders and academics. They are viewed as subcontractors for projects in Africa, competing with local NGOs and civil-society organisations and the private sector for funds and activities; as sponsors of political crises; as 'spies' for their home countries; and as job seekers. Their contribution to the host countries' economic growth has not been verified by quantitative evaluations.

'Spies' for their home countries?

Governments in Africa are frequently suspicious of INGOs. There have been government claims that these organisations' foreign, and even local, employees work as spies. There are claims that these organisations work closely with political or military 'rebels'. It is claimed that they fund the opposition. There are claims that these organisations have 'infiltrated' Africa's high offices (as Mbeki said[6]) and are doing not charity or humanitarian work, but spying on regimes. There are claims that they have access to the people at the top (such as army generals, the police, judiciary, members of parliament, senior civil servants and ministers). In some cases their agenda may be in the interests of foreign communities and may not be wholly in the interests of the African host country. It is claimed they also influence people at grass roots by funding community-based organisations (CBOs). And this may not be happening just in Africa alone. New evidence shows that Russia was spied on by NGOs funded from outside. In January 2006, Russia caught the UK spying on it using a 'fake rock'. The UK flatly denied the claim. Recently, Tony Blair's aide, Jonathan Powell, then Prime Minister Tony Blair's chief of staff, told a BBC documentary it was 'embarrassing', but 'they had us bang to rights'.[7] This means that it was true that the UK was spying on Russia.

The Russian security services alleged that British security services had been making covert payments to the opposition and NGOs. They seem to have linked this spying to the NGOs, which were getting money from outside the country. So shortly after making the allegations, President Putin introduced a law restricting NGOs from getting funding from foreign governments. Many closed down as a result. Alluding to why he had put in place this law, Putin said: 'We have seen attempts by the secret services to make use of NGOs. NGOs have been financed through secret service channels. No one can deny that this money stinks.'

Job seekers?

Some argue that foreign governments create jobs for their nationals working in NGOs in Africa and other parts of the world. Almost all the INGOs that work in Africa have top management occupied by foreigners from the countries where these organisations are headquartered and were originally established, or from those countries that fund these INGOs. The personnel are paid well, at times more than they would be paid at home with their level of experience and qualifications. It is argued that INGO staff work as advisors in Africa, but do not have the appropriate experience and qualifications to do so.

Quantitative evaluations of NGO work

Quantitative evaluations of NGOs are non-existent. However, there are some academic studies that have estimated the effects of individual projects and have found that some projects had positive outcomes. For example, projects in education in Kenya and India have been shown to improve educational outcomes (Banerjee et al., 2003; Kremer, 2003). However, other randomised evaluations[8] of NGO programmes have found that they made no difference to the lives of the people who were the intended beneficiaries. Other writers have been critical of INGOs' role of capacity building of local and grass roots organisations.

What is positive is that when their programme terms expire, some INGO experts stay on in the countries of their projects. They settle down and sometimes start families. This way, former INGO managers help reduce poverty in a personal capacity by contributing to national wealth and GDP, having become citizens of their host country.

INGOs have big budgets that are never open to public scrutiny. They never give accountability to the poor, disadvantaged or vulnerable that they claim their work benefits. They never even account to the public in their home countries. Unlike private-sector companies, they never publish their financial statements in the media. They only present project reports (with expenditure) to their funders. Do these organisations fear accountability?[9] That we may never know.

Local organisations, with their experience in advocacy and awareness creation, have developed appetites for politics.[10] In fact, some of them are more vocal than political parties in some countries, such as Uganda and Kenya. Governments in Africa are aware that such organisations have the money to support those who oppose the leaders in power. Unfortunately, this is hard to either defend or ignore. Their advocacy agenda can be viewed at times as regime-change initiatives.

Staffers in local and international NGOs may have some political agenda to achieve in the near future. In Kenya, those NGO personnel who used to advocate regime change during President Daniel Arap Moi's time got their rewards. They became part of the new government after Moi.

These organisations usually have at least three layers of employees. The first layer directly serves the headquarters at home. The second layer includes a closely selected group of individuals in charge of press relations. These are mainly Africans, at times nationals of the country in which they are hired to work. They are locals who have usually studied near (or done their internships at) the headquarters of these organisations for which they are now working, and they are usually paid better than the country's civil servants or other local colleagues. The last group is the rest of the staff in the organisation, including sometimes even those small local NGOs which receive financial support from the INGO. The function of these employees is to receive and implement instructions. They may not critically analyse the motives of their seniors. They may demonstrate; and they may get shot in action.

Can these organisations support fact-based research or research and development in the countries where they operate? The argument has always been that there is enough research conducted worldwide on Africa available in London, Washington, New York,

and Berlin, for example. With regard to performance, most publicly available programme evaluations by NGOs, such as case
studies, are of a qualitative nature, and rarely contain rigorous
statistical analysis, and they almost never report strong negative
outcomes (Werker & Ahmed, 2008). Many researchers continue
to look at Africa as one large country with similar problems. So
if there was research done in the DRC, the assumption is this
research will also be relevant to the conditions in Zimbabwe, or
another African country.

There is another recent view emerging from the EU former
commissioner, which could support the African view of the role of
NGOs. He has implied that European NGOs have some agenda to
keep Africa in poverty. Lord Peter Mandelson, former EU trade
commissioner and UK secretary of state for business, told The
Times Africa CEO Africa Summit in London that European NGOs
opposed his attempts to renegotiate trade agreements that would
afford Africa more commercial opportunities.[11] Coming from such
a high-profile personality could also lend some credence to what
African governments and some academics are saying.

INGOs competing with local NGOs

Most countries in Africa have local NGOs and civil-society organisations. These are non-governmental; they are not private-sector
entities; their mandate is to help the poor and the vulnerable.
There are organisations that lobby for fair aid, and of late a few
advocate fair and just trade rules, and social and economic justice. There are others working on basic human rights. There are
several issues that have to be looked at when considering these
organisations.

The local organisations that are genuinely local and promote a
pro-development agenda have to contend with competition from
INGOs in their work. They have to ensure that they are vocal and

visible because the INGOs' visibility is based on their large budgets and their country of origin. To succeed, local organisations have to cooperate with INGOs. It is not uncommon to find that certain local organisations that have their own budgets and are funded by donors are persuaded to accept small amounts of funding from INGOs. They may accept a very meagre deposit of cash for a one-off activity. This is because they have to work with the big brother. Some NGOs may get funding from the INGOs that work on relief, disaster or humanitarian programmes in order to undertake advocacy work. These are the most vulnerable to the competition from the INGOs. They cannot undertake any activity without consulting the funders, the INGOs. At times, they will be told that this activity is expensive or irrelevant only to find out that the INGO has taken over the very activity they had been advised against. When the INGOs find that an issue is sensitive and requires a local voice, they will pressurise the local NGOs to speak on their behalf.

And in return, the INGOs give them very little money as funding for this big and risky service,[12] money they can't refuse. How can they refuse it when part of it pays the small salaries in countries where unemployment is more than 40 per cent? How much do the so-called INGO experts earn? Much more than nationals.

How independent are local NGOs and civil-society organisations?

Then there are the think tanks, which regard themselves as independent, with an agenda to investigate and use evidence-based information to help influence the pro-poor public policies. One can look at independence from various angles. These organisations have their own strategic plans, staff and boards. The board annually approves their work plan and budget. Maybe, however, this is where their independence starts and stops. To approve funding, the funders must agree the work and agenda of the recipient. Therefore, local organisations are supposed to help the international organisations achieve their agenda. In which case, is the recipient really independent from the donor? It should be mentioned that some local think tanks' and NGOs' donors include INGOs – either directly from their country office headquarters or their cooperating members. Have you ever wondered why an organisation that started working on aid effectiveness ended on climate change, justice or women's rights? The funders influence the agenda, they tell the local organisation to follow their new funding thematic area if they want to continue working with them.

NGOs and Africa's growth and development

Any key stakeholder or partner will realise that it is lack of sustained growth that has created high levels of absolute poverty in Africa. This means that all these stakeholders need to focus on the major challenges. People in Africa require cheap sources of credit, quality education, products for local and export markets, access to lucrative markets, and infrastructure and institutions that support markets. In a coffee-producing region, for example, the local community should be helped to produce more coffee and sell it successfully.

When trying to lobby for market access and market entry, and a just and fair trade system[13] with the developed and advanced economies, stakeholders should do local research and identify the challenges. Most presentations in trade meetings, for example, tend to be based on the experience of India and its challenges. However, the problems experienced by Africa's developing countries are not the same as those in India or other advanced developing countries, such as Brazil or Argentina. China and India are referred to as developing countries, just like Zambia and Malawi. But Zambia and Malawi are not among the advanced developing countries. Most countries in sub-Saharan Africa are less developed. Furthermore, the challenges of these different countries are unique. For instance, India may have at least 100 million poor people, but it is also a growing economy and an advanced country with high levels of technology. It also faces different market access and entry challenges from the EU or US markets, which are not the same as those of Malawi and Zambia. This, therefore, necessitates research that pays attention to the particular countries. Ironically, this is rarely the case. INGOs that have money for relief work should work with government on such projects to help realise effective inputs for development.

There are two schools of thought on NGO work and government. The dominant one is that NGOs should not work with government, or support or advise it. The second view, often opposed by INGOs, is that if you want to help the people, then you should work with their government. What is clear is that it is not necessary or advisable to be confrontational to government. Taking the time to provide advice and support for government may be more helpful. And INGOs should let government know how they want to provide support. It is not impossible to support government's efforts without becoming compromised. After all, the budget comes from abroad.

Conclusion

The image of Africa is not good. It is not good inside the continent, where the local press has done a lot to sully its image. It is not good overseas either, and the foreign press has not helped. They visit to film the worst slums, ignoring the new, modern urban developments. They look forward to interviewing politicians and heads of NGOs about failure of governance and poor accountability. Pictures in the international media show emaciated children or child soldiers. TV stations run documentaries about Idi Amin of Uganda and Mobutu of Zaire – stories that happened decades ago.

There is a need to tell the good stories, too, the African success stories. There are many developments across the continent that are raising Africa to a higher level of growth. Yet the way Africa and Africans are perceived by the rest of the world perpetuates the negative image. Some of the present author's own personal experiences illustrate this.

In 1998 in Lisbon, Portugal, a lady visited the Ugandan stand at the Lisboa Expo98. She asked the present author, how is Idi Amin? Amin left Uganda in 1979. In June 1999 the author was at Schiphol Airport, Amsterdam, where a man approached him and said, 'Leave our country and stop begging from us.'

In August 2000, he was in Germany. He attempted to pay for some items in a chain store with his German bank card. They refused to accept the debit card, and insisted on cash. The author asked to see the manager. When the author showed him his ID with the words *Aus Amt* and the German national bird symbol, signifying diplomatic status, the manager instructed his staff to accept the card, which they did, albeit grudgingly.

In 2002, while visiting Canada, he was asked whether he had ever lived in a tree. And the question was not put to him by children. And whenever he told work colleagues at the end of assignments that he would be returning to his home country, Uganda, the frequent response was that he should not go back, and that he would be killed and eaten by people in Africa.

The author was once rerouted at Gatwick via Charles de Gaulle Airport, Paris, on his way to Italy to promote Ugandan trade in the 1990s. Why was he rerouted even though he had a transit visa and transfer to the other terminal? The only conclusion he can reach was that being young and African, he would be able to enter the UK and 'disappear' there – become an illegal immigrant, and a burden on the British public coffers.

And in the 1990s, while the author was in Amsterdam, an elderly man approached and offered him a few guilders.

What these different stories illustrate is that there is much ignorance about this beautiful continent trying to rise out of poverty. Just as I have illustrated with these real-life stories, Africans are perceived as having problems. This is a mentality that has to stop. Africans have to resolve these problems and reverse the negative imagery themselves in the various ways presented in this book. They have to end the beggar mentality. They have to say no to hand-outs. They have to work hard to achieve success. Governments have to draw up strategies to eliminate poverty. Countries and entities giving aid or donations have to stop. They should instead encourage Africa to trade; their support should be in the form of trade, not aid. African countries need improved, sustained economic growth so that its people are not viewed as beggars and problems, but contributors to world prosperity. After all, Africa has a concentration of natural resources – oil, diamonds, gold, coltan, uranium, natural forests, freshwater lakes and rivers.

We have seen in this book that there are various problems Africa faces and various factors that account for Africa's growth failure. However, economic progress and development in Africa are possible. Africa's poor economies can eradicate poverty and achieve and sustain higher levels of economic growth. There are already some star performers in sub-Saharan Africa, such as Botswana, Mauritius, Uganda and, lately, Ghana (after it began producing oil), that can be regarded as pathfinders.

As discussed in this book, there are many views, theories and hypotheses about what have been Africa's causes of failure to sustain growth. These include predominantly internal factors, such as the continent's geography, the nature of African leaders, ethnic conflict, weak civil society, pandemic diseases, failure of democracy, the oil rentier-state mentality; rampant corruption; unfavourable trade relations with the developed world; and entrenched cultural practices. Despite these factors, others still continue to blame Africa's economic failure on the impact of colonialism.

Other writers have stated that the solutions to the African question entail wealthy nations ceasing to give aid and Africa ceasing to accept it; selling government bonds as a way to a capital solution; and trade. The purpose of this book has not been to indicate the main cause of failure. What this book has shown is that Africa's challenges are principally internal and stem from the failure to sustain rapid economic growth, and that sustained economic growth would spread the benefits of quantity and quality for the markets, and enhance economic development. The steps in the right direction towards enhancing sustained economic growth include government efforts to encourage every family to become part of the market's production and supply chain; improving the quality of what is produced; adding value to exports; keeping savings in banks; attracting meaningful and serious investments (with joint ventures with the local entities); drafting good laws on immigration and labour, and enforcing them (foreigners who come as investors should not become street vendors and hawkers, for example). Added to these is the vitality of international relations and image building. When trade strategies are prepared well and implemented as part of the whole national development plan, trade can become a catalyst for economic development. The role of African governments in this globalised era is to provide infrastructure development, boost the key sectors that generate ample revenue, set up institutions that support private-sector development, identify key sectors for joint public-private-sector investment and undertake campaigns aimed at promoting the importance of markets and trading.

Africans themselves must understand that they have to take the initiative to develop. They should invest in relevant education and training, send their people abroad to learn and become technically-minded, attract investments and finally choose prosperity.

But the wealthy countries of the West also have a part to play in the upliftment process. The new role rich countries should adopt is to focus on advocating free and open markets in their countries for products from Africa; halting the inflow of dirty money from Africa; supporting the gradual development of democracy efforts; partnering in infrastructural development; and rethinking the contribution to growth and development that could be made by NGOs (which currently tend to be advocacy- and not production-oriented). This is all that rich countries and their people can and should do.

As has been seen recently in the Arab region of North Africa, democracy is preceded by growth. Democracy may have to follow economic development. People who are hungry cannot demonstrate for weeks in the streets. How will their families survive while the breadwinner is engaged in demonstrating against the government? There is still a long way to go.

Acknowledgements

To wife my Aggie K and children KK and AK;
and to my parents;
and to Annex, Martin, Shady, Darius and Agatha.

I dedicate this book to the many peasants in
rural Africa without a future.

I would like to thank Gerhard Mulder for his tireless
effort and encouragement on this project.
Thank you to Kristin Paremoer and Mark Ronan,
and to Sam Alioni, my IT support.

References

Colonialism and the slave trade: Their impact on African economies

Acemoglu, D., Johnson, S. & Robinson, J.A., 2002. Reversal of fortune: Geography and institutions in the making of the modern world income distribution. *The Quarterly Journal of Economics* 117 (4): 1231–1294.

Manning, P., 1990. *Slavery and African Life*. Cambridge: Cambridge University Press.

Moyo, D. 2009. *Dead Aid*. London: Penguin.

Nunn, N., 2003. *The Legacy of Colonialism: A Model of Africa's Underdevelopment*. University of Toronto occasional paper, June 2003.

Sejjaaka, S., 2004. A political and economic history of Uganda, 1962–2002. In Bird, F. & Herman, S., 2004. *International Business and the Challenges of Poverty in Developing Areas*. Palgrave-Macmillan.

Wa Thiong'o, N. 1993. *Moving the Centre: The Struggle for Cultural Freedom*. London: Heinemann.

Colonisation: No longer an excuse for Africa's current poor economic performance

Achebe, C., 1984. *The Trouble with Nigeria*. Heinemann (1984), reissued by Fourth Dimension Publishing (2000).

Agrawal, P., Sahoo, P. & Kumar Dash, R., 2007. *Savings Behaviour in South Asia*, paper presented at the National Conference on Expanding Freedom: Towards Social and Economic Transformation in a Globalising World, April 11–13, Delhi, Institute of Economic Growth. *Proceedings* 93(2): 102–115.

Collier, P. & Hoeffler, A., 2004. *The Challenge of Reducing the Global Incidence of Civil War*. Oxford University: Copenhagen Consensus Challenge Paper.

Cyril, O., 2009. Nigeria's Niger Delta: Understanding the complex drivers of violent oil-related conflict. *Africa Development* XXXIV (2). Council for the Development of Social Science Research in Africa.

Duesberg, P.H., 1996. *Inventing the Aids virus*. Washington D.C.: Regnery Publishing.

Easley, L-E., 2007. Correlates of nationalism and implications for security in East Asia. *Issues and Insights* 7(10): 3–8. P.1.

Easterly, W. & Levine, R., 1997. Africa's growth tragedy: Policies and ethnic divisions. *Quarterly Journal of Economics*: 1203–1250.

Huntington, S.P., 1991. *The Third Wave: Democratisation in the late 20th Century*. Norman: University of Oklahoma Press.

Huntington, S.P. 1999. Keynote address, *Cultures in the 21st Century: Conflicts and convergences*. Colorado College's 125th Anniversary Symposium, 4 February 1999. See http://coloradocollege.edu/Academics/Anniversary/Transcripts/ HuntingtonTXT.htm (accessed on 4 October 2010).

Kamppeter, W., 2008. *Dictatorship, Democracy and Economic Regime Reflections on the Experience of South Korea*. Frederich Ebbert Stiftung Korea, www.library. fes.de/pdf-files/iez/05399.pdf (accessed 10 January 2012).

Mapuva, J. & Chari, F., 2010. Colonialism no longer an excuse for Africa's failure. *Journal of Sustainable Development in Africa* 12(5).

McKinsey Global Institute, 2010. *Lions on the Move: The Progress and Potential of African Economies*.

Miller, S.C., Spakerdas, S., Soares, R., & Willman, A. (2009). *The Costs of Violence*. Social Development Department, World Bank. Washington D.C.: World Bank.

Mugenyi, P., 2008. *Genocide by Denial: How Profiteering from HIV/AIDS Killed Millions*. Fountain Publishers.

Narayan, D. & Petesch, P., 2002. *Voices of the Poor: From Many Lands* (vol. 30). Washington D.C.: World Bank and Oxford University Press.

Nkrumah, K., 1961. *I speak of freedom*. London: Heinemann.

Satyanath, M. & Sergenti, E., 2004. Economic shocks and civil conflict: An instrumental variables approach. *Journal of Political Economy* 112: 725–753.

Sen, A., 2004. How does culture matter? In Rao & Walton (Eds), 2004. *Culture and Public Action*. Stanford University Press.

UBOS (Uganda Bureau of Statistics), 2009. Spatial trends of poverty and inequality in Uganda. Kampala: UBOS.

UNAIDS, World Health Organisation, 2009. *Aids Epidemic Update: 2009*. Geneva: UNAIDS.

Van Lierde, J. (ed.), 1972. *Lumumba speaks: The speeches and writings of Patrice Lumumba 1958-1961*. Boston: Little, Brown and Company.

Vogel, E., 2004. The rise of China and the changing face of East Asia. *Asia-Pacific Review* 11(1): 46–57.

Committed leadership or multi-party democracy?

Barro, R.J., 1996. Democracy and Growth. *Journal of Economic Growth* 1(1): 1–27.

Barro, R.J., 1999. Determinants of Democracy. *Journal of Political Economy* 107 (6): 2.

Bui, C., 2010. Mass attitudes towards democracy in different regimes: Testing an assumption in democratic qualities. APSA Annual Meeting, Washington DC, September 2010.

Moyo, D., 2009. *Dead Aid*. London: Penguin.

The private sector and managing resources

Stiglitz, J.E., 2002. *Globalisation and its Discontents*. New York: W.W. Norton.

Takebe, M. & York, R.C., 2011. External sustainability of oil-producing sub-Saharan African countries. IMF Working Paper, WP/11/207, August 2011, http://www.imf.org/external/pubs/ft/wp/2011/wp11207.pdf (accessed on 21 January 2012).

Effect of corruption on economic growth and development

African Economic Outlook 2011, http://www.africaneconomicoutlook.org/en/data-statistics/ (accessed on 24 January 2012).

Ayittey, G., 2010. The worst of the worst. *Foreign Policy*, July/August 2010.

Ayittey, G., 2010. The worst of the worst revisited. *Foreign Policy*, 9 September 2011.

Gbenga, L., 2007. Corruption and development in Africa: Challenges for political and economic change. *Humanity & Social Sciences Journal* 2(1): 1–7.

Henriot, J.P., 2007. *Corruption in Zambia: Is it inevitable? Can we stop it?* Presentation in JCTR 2007 Series, Alliance Française, Lusaka, 19 April 2007.

IMF (International Monetary Fund), 2000. *Improving Governance and Fighting Corruption in the Baltic and CIS Countries*, July, http://www.imf.org/external/pubs/ft/issues/issues21/index.htm (accessed on 3 June 2011).

Lerrick, A., 2005. *Aid to Africa at Risk: Covering Up Corruption*. Carnegie Mellon Gailliot Center for Public Policy International Economics Report, December.

Ogundiya, I.S., 2010. Corruption: The bane of democratic stability in Nigeria. *Current Research Journal of Social Sciences* 2(4): 233–241. Maxwell Scientific Organisation.

Transparency International, 2011. *Corruption Perceptions Index 2011: The perceived levels of public-sector corruption in 183 countries/territories around the world*. Transparency International.

Population strategies and educating the people

African Economic Outlook, 2011, http://www.africaneconomicoutlook.org/en/data-statistics/ (accessed on 20 January 2012).

Bloom, D.E. & Canning, D., 2000. The health and wealth of nations. *Science* 287(5456): 1207–1209.

Bloom, D., Canning, D. & Malaney, P., 2000. Demographic change and economic growth in Asia. *Population and Development Review* 26: 257–290.

Bloom, D.E., Canning, D. & Sevilla, J., 2003. *The demographic dividend: A new perspective on the economic consequences of population change.* Rand Publishing.

Bloom, D.E. & Williamson, J.G., 1998. Demographic transitions and economic miracles in emerging Asia. *World Bank Economic Review* 12(3): 419–456.

Bongaarts J., 1998. *Dependency burdens in the developing world.* Population Council, New York.

Fairbanks, M. & Lindsay, S., 1997. *Plowing the sea: Nurturing the hidden sources of growth in the developing countries.* Harvard Business Press.

Morrell, R., Bhana, D. & Shefer, T. (eds), 2011. *Books and babies: Pregnancy and young parents in schools,* HSRC Press.

Tabaire, B. 2011. One citizen's 2011 resolutions. *Saturday Monitor,* 1 January 2011.

UBOS, 2009 (Uganda Bureau of Statistics). Statistical Abstract, 2009. UBOS.

UNECA (United Nations Economic Commission for Africa), 2010. *Economic report on Africa 2010: Promoting high-level sustainable growth to reduce unemployment in Africa.* Addis Ababa: UNECA.

UNECA, 2011. *African youth report: Addressing the youth education and employment nexus in the new global economy.* Addis Ababa: UNECA.

UNESCO Institute of Statistics, 2011. *Financing education in sub-Saharan Africa: Meeting the challenges of expansion, equity and quality.* UNESCO-UIS.

Wang Feng, 2005. Can China afford to continue its one-child policy? *Asia Pacific Issue, Analysis from the East-West Center* 77, March.

WHO (World Health Organisation), 2001. Commission on Macroeconomics and Health. *Macroeconomics and health: Investing in health for economic development.* Geneva: WHO.

William E. 2006. *The white man's burden: Why the West's efforts to aid the rest have done so much ill and so little good.* Penguin Press.

World Bank, 2011. Africa development indicators factoids 2011, http://siteresources. worldbank.org/INTAFRICA/Resources/Africa-factoids_hi-res_FINAL_ Sept_9-2011_11.pdf (accessed 10 January 2012).

The informal sector and tools for attracting investment

African Development Bank, 2011. *Africa in 50 years' time: The road towards inclusive growth.* Tunis: African Development Bank.

Allen, F., Otchere, I. & Senbet, L.W., 2010. *African Financial Systems: A Review*. The Wharton School, University of Pennsylvania.

Bates, R.H., 1981. *Markets and States in Tropical Africa: The Political Basis of Agricultural Policies*. Berkeley: University of California Press.

Becker, K.F., 2004. *The Informal Economy: Fact-Finding Study*. Swedish International Development Agency (SIDA).

Birdsall, N., 2010. *The (indispensable) middle class in developing countries; or, the rich and the rest, not the poor and the rest*. CGD Working Paper 207. Washington, D.C.: Center for Global Development.

Birdsall, N., Graham, C. & Pettinato, S., 2000. *Stuck in the tunnel: Is globalisation muddling the middle class?* Center on Social and Economic Dynamics, Working Paper No. 14, August.

De Soto, H., 2000. *The Mystery of Capital: Why Capitalism Triumphs in the West and Fails Everywhere Else*. New York: Basic Books.

Fairbanks, M. & Lindsay, S., 1997. *Plowing the Sea: Nurturing the Hidden Sources of Growth in the Developing Countries*. Harvard Business Press.

FAO, 2004. *Land Tenure and Administration in Africa: Lessons Of Experience and Emerging Issues*. Prepared by Cotula, L. FAO.

Fiess, N., Fugazza, M. & Maloney, W.F., 2006. *Informal labor markets and macroeconomic fluctuations*. Mimeo, World Bank.

Friedman, M., 1962. *Capitalism and Freedom*. Chicago: University of Chicago Press.

ILO (International Labour Organisation), 2002. *Globalisation and the Informal Economy: How Global Trade and Investment Impact on the Working Poor*. Geneva: ILO.

Landes, D., 1998. *The Wealth and Poverty of Nations: Why Some are So Rich and Some So Poor*. New York: W.W. Norton & Company.

Malthus, Rev. T., 1798. *An Essay on the Principle of Population – As it Affects the Future Improvement of Society*. London: J. Johnson, St. Paul's Churchyard.

Moyo, D., 2009. *Dead Aid*. London: Penguin.

Porter, M., 1990. *The Competitive Advantage of Nations*. The Free Press.

Schneider, F., 2007. Shadow economies and corruption all over the world: new estimates for 145 countries. Open Access, *Open Assessment E-Journal* 2009(9), 24 July.

Shaohua, C. & Martin, R., 2008. *The Developing World is Poorer Than We Thought, But No Less Successful in the Fight against Poverty*. Policy Research Working Paper 4703. World Bank, August.

Shinn, S., 2009. Human side of finance. *Biz Ed*, July/August.

Skidelsky, R., 1992. *John Maynard Keynes: The Economist as Saviour*. London: Penguin Books.

World Bank, 2011. *Sub-Saharan Africa, Global Economic Prospects, June 2011: Regional Annex*, http://siteresources.worldbank.org/INTGEP/Resources/ 335315-1307471336123/7983902-1307479336019/AFR-Annex.pdf (accessed on 22 January 2012).

World Bank & African Development Bank, 2011. *Leveraging Migration for Africa: Remittances, Skills, and Investments, 2010.*

Regional and international trade relations

Brautigam, D., 2011 (2009). *The dragon's gift: The real story of China in Africa.* Oxford: Oxford University Press.

Brautigam, D., 2011. *China in Africa: What can Western donors learn?* Norfund.

Cheung, Y.-W., De Haan, J. & Shu Yu, 2011. China's outward direct investment in Africa. Hong Kong Institute For Monetary Research, *Working Paper No. 13/2011*, April.

Schiere, R. & Rugamba, A., 2011. Chinese infrastructure investments and African integration. African Development Bank, *Working Paper Series, No. 127*, May.

Access to markets and 'just and fair' trade

Chang, H.-J., 2002. *Kicking away the ladder: Development strategy in a historical perspective.* London: Anthem Press.

Chang, H.-J., 2007. *Bad Samaritans: Rich nations and the threat to the developing world.* London: Random House.

Konrad Adenauer Stiftung, *Pro-poor development and poverty reduction in Uganda and the idea of social market economy*, http://www.kas.de/uganda/en/publications/29764/ (accessed on 15 January 2012).

Krugman, P. & Obstfeld, M., 2003. *International economics: Theory and policies*, 6th edition. Addison Wesley.

Rana, K., 2000. *Inside diplomacy.* New Delhi: Manas.

Sachs, J.D., 2005. *The end of poverty: How we can make it happen in our life time?* Penguin.

Tang, H. & Harrison, H., 2005. Liberalisation of trade: Why so much controversy? In World Bank, 2005. *Economic growth in the 1990s: Learning from a decade of reform.*

Twineyo-Kamugisha, E. 2011. *Pro-poor development and poverty reduction in Uganda and the idea of social market economy.* Paper presented at the high-level roundtable discussion organised by the African Centre for Trade and Development with support from the Konrad Adenauer-Stiftung.

Are international NGOs promoting Africa's economic growth?

Banerjee, A., Cole, S., Duflo, E. & Linden, L., 2003. *Improving the quality of education in India: Evidence from three randomized experiments.* Centre for Policy Research;

Barr, A., Fafchamps, M. & Owens, T., 2005. The governance of non-governmental organizations in Uganda. *World Development* 33(4): 657–679, April.

Chang, H.-J., 2002. *Kicking away the ladder: Development strategy in a historical perspective.* London: Anthem Press.

Cohen, M.A., Küpçü, M.F. & Khanna, P. 2008. The new colonialists. *Foreign Policy*, July/August.

Duflo, E. & Kremer, M., 2003. *Use of randomization in the evaluation of development effectiveness.* Paper prepared for the World Bank Operations Evaluation Department Conference on Evaluation and Development Effectiveness. Washington, 15–16 July 2003.

Fisher, W.F., 1997. Doing good? The politics and antipolitics of NGO practices. *Annual Review of Anthropology*, 26: 439–464.

Hulme, D. & Edwards, M., 1997. *Too close for comfort?: NGOs, states and donors.* London: Macmillan.

Kremer, M., 2003. Randomized evaluations of educational programs in developing countries: Some lessons. *American Economic Review Papers and Proceedings* 93(2): 102–115.

Stiles, K., 2002. International support for NGOs in Bangladesh: Some unintended consequences. *World Development* 30(5): 835–846.

Werker, E.D, & Ahmed, F. Z. (2008). What do nongovernmental organizations do? Journal of Economic Perspectives, 22(2), 73–92.

Zivetz, L., 1991. *Doing good: The Australian NGO community.* North Sydney: Allen & Unwin.

Notes

Colonialism and the slave trade: Their impact on African economies

1 Those traditional rulers who opposed selling fellow Africans and colonisation had their kingdoms or chiefdoms punished severely; their leaders were exiled or killed. This befell the King of the Bunyoro Kingdom in Uganda. Its king, Kabalega, was later forced out of his kingdom and exiled in the Seychelles.

2 Within Africa, under kings and chiefs, slaves were employed in many ways as servants, concubines, soldiers, administrators and fieldworkers. In some cases, as in the ancient empire of Ghana and in Kongo, there were whole villages of enslaved dependants were required to pay tribute to the ruler. See http://history-world.org/Africa%20in%20the%20age%20of%20the%20slave%20trade.htm (accessed 22 May 2012).

3 On the initiative of Portugal, Bismarck, the German chancellor, invited representatives of Austria-Hungary, Belgium, Denmark, France, the UK, Italy, the Netherlands, Portugal, Russia, Spain, Sweden-Norway (which was a union until 1905), the Ottoman Empire and the US to take part in the Berlin Conference to partition Africa. Details of the 1884 Berlin Conference can be found at http://en.wikipedia.org/wiki/Berlin_Conference_(1884) (accessed 4 March 2010).

4 The Samia are another such ethnic group. Some live in Uganda; others are across the border in Kenya.

5 The British colonialists used the Baganda to subdue and conquer other parts of Uganda. In return, Buganda got sound infrastructure, education, social services and the capital city. At independence, in 1962, Buganda was granted a semi-autonomous position within the state of Uganda. Four years later, this led to friction between the central government and the king of Buganda. The repercussion was the abolition of monarchies by premier Milton Obote in 1966 and the establishment of a Uganda as a republic.

6 Ngugi wa Thiong'o (1993: 78) captures it well: 'First it has been the external factor of foreign invasion, occupation, and control, and second, the internal factor of collaboration with the external threat.'

7 Museveni asserts that ancient Egypt was conquered for the first time in 525–532 BC by Darius from Asia Minor (present-day Turkey) because the latter had developed iron technology while the former were still using brass, a much weaker metal. The articles in which Museveni explains Egypt and its black people can be found at http://www.newvision.co.ug/D/8/459/527022 (accessed 10 March 2010) and http://www.newvision.co.ug/D/120/132/726786 (accessed 10 March 2010).

8 The kingdom of Bunyoro-Kitara suffered the wrath of the British for their stubbornness and refusal to accept imperial rule. Once the most powerful kingdom in East Africa, and extending to parts of Uganda, Tanzania, Rwanda and Zaire, its powerful king, Kabalega, was exiled and the king's people decimated.

Colonisation: No longer an excuse for Africa's current poor economic performance

1 These are the countries that have experienced lack of sustained growth and have high levels of poverty, some with over 30 per cent of the population living below the poverty line (i.e. less than $1 a day). The World Bank lists 47 developing countries in Africa as sub-Saharan Africa, see http://data. worldbank.org/about/country-classifications/country-and-lending-groups#Sub_Saharan_Africa (accessed on 12 July 2011).

2 The *Economic Report on Africa 2010*, published by UNECA, states that although accurate data on poverty in Africa are hard to come by, there is evidence that poverty rates are high and rising. In 2005, the proportion of people living in extreme poverty, using the new $1.25 per day poverty line, was 51 per cent in sub-Saharan Africa.

3 When people want to show respect to Mandela, they address him as Madiba. When South Africa was selected to host the 2010 World Cup, the first ever in Africa, in excitement, then President Mbeki said that this was a moment of Madiba magic.

4 He is likely to be beatified by the Pope soon; if so, he will become the first politician of our time to be made a saint.

5 *Ujaama* means oneness, unity or togetherness.

6 See http://www.bbc.co.uk/worldservice/people/highlights/000914_nkrumah. shtml (accessed on 14 January 2012).

7 See http://www.bbc.co.uk/worldservice/people/highlights/000914_nkrumah. shtml (accessed on 14 January 2012).

8 Ibid.

9 John R. Stockwell is a former CIA officer who became a critic of US government policies after serving in the agency for 13 years in seven tours of duty. After managing US involvement in the Angolan Civil War as chief of the Angola Task Force during its 1975 covert operations, he resigned and wrote *In Search of Enemies*, the only detailed insider's account of a major CIA covert action. See http://en.wikipedia.org/wiki/John_Stockwell (accessed on 10 January 2012).

10 British government documents, recently declassified under the 30-year rule, have supported earlier accounts by the journalists Pat Hutton and Jonathan Bloch, which said the rise of Idi Amin was engineered by outside interests to stop President Milton Obote's nationalisation drive in which the state had taken 60 per cent interest in all foreign and Ugandan Asian-owned businesses (http://www.africasia.com/archive/na/01_02/cover2.htm). While attend-

ing the Commonwealth heads of state conference in Singapore in 1971, Obote opposed British arms sales to apartheid South Africa, to which the British prime minister, Edward Heath, responded with a veiled threat that he may not return to his country. Later Obote was informed that there had been a military coup and Amin had taken over. Obote was aware that the internal situation in Uganda was not good, but went to the conference at the behest of President Nyerere of Tanzania, who wanted to present opposition to the British government's arms sales to South Africa.

11 See http://gulfcoastjewishfamilyandcommunityservices.org/refugee/files/ 2011/04/CCR-congo.pdf (accessed on 13 January 2012).

12 See http://people.hofstra.edu/alan_j_singer/CoursePacks/PatriceLumumba-andtheStruggleforAfricanIndependence.pdf (accessed on 13 January 2012).

13 The Belgian government officially apologised in 2002 for the execution of Lumumba.

14 The author considers that the term 'tribe' refers pejoratively to people in pre-developed societies. It was used to refer to the African and Native American communities by those who colonised them. There are no white 'tribes' in the US or the UK, for example. The author's preferred term is 'community' or 'ethnic group'.

15 Dr Besigye, opposition presidential candidate in Uganda, 2011, said: 'Maybe many of you have not had a chance to move to other parts of the country because those people think that for you are very well-off . . . Those people from other parts of the country are so angry that it is only you who have benefited from Museveni's 25-year rule. They think that you are so rich yet you are also poor like them.' (Place country above tribe, *Daily Monitor*, 4 February 2011, http://www.monitor.co.ug/SpecialReports/Elections/-/859108/ 1101362/-/k2dwwn/-/index.html.) (Accessed 3 June 2012.)

16 In Uganda, there have been claims that since 1986, the western region is enjoying a bigger portion of the country's wealth. What is clear is that there are disparities in employment in Africa caused by favouritism and nepotism, and that such disparities cause resentment, hatred and unrest. For those who want more evidence about the ethnic division and development from researchers who documented the evidence, see Narayan and Petesch (2002).

17 In 2011, a new country was established in Africa when south Sudan seceded: the Republic of South Sudan.

18 In Uganda, for example, the Baganda ethnic group view themselves more as Bagandan than Ugandan and would like their king to hold political power. They have continued to demand federal status from government, without

success. They do not regard themselves as Ugandans. This creates problems with other ethnic groups in Uganda, because the Baganda consider themselves superior; they live in the central region, home to the capital, which is also the political capital. They were also the first to meet the Europeans and to request Christian missionaries. They believe this makes them superior to other Ugandans.

19 http://hdr.undp.org/en/media/HDR_2010_EN_Table1_reprint.pdf (accessed 22 January 2012); see also siteresources.worldbank.org/DATA-STATISTICS/ . . . /GNIPC.pdf (accessed on 22 January 2012).

20 See http://www.gallup.com/poll/145787/sub-saharan-africans-struggle-financially-even-gdp-grows.aspx (accessed on 22 January 2012).

21 Nationalism is a manifestation of national identity: a consciousness of belonging to a particular national group with distinguishing characteristics. National identity, a product of human psychology, is contingent on historical interpretation and constructed through social interaction. As a result, national identity varies across cases and its expression in nationalist behaviour is a necessarily political process. See Easley (2007: 1).

22 According to Vogel (2004), generations of Chinese have dreamt of making their country rich and powerful since the time of the Opium War (also known as the Anglo-Chinese War – 1839–1842).

23 Details of the interview can found at Al Jazeera: http://english.aljazeera.net/news/africa/2011/01/2011171839053529.html (accessed 20 July 2011).

24 Although the rebel group led by Joseph Kony claimed it wanted to establish a theocratic state based on the Ten Commandments, in reality it was mainly based on ethnic tendencies.

25 For further information, see Paul Collier and Anke Hoeffler, who have conducted a great deal of research on war, conflict and violence in Africa. Some of their articles are available in the references section.

26 Scholars such as Paul Collier, William Easterly and Levine found evidence to support the fact that the ethnic diversity has negative consequences for growth and creates a higher incidence of war or conflict, especially in Africa. Easterly and Levine (1997) have found that the aggregate level of ethnic diversity significantly reduces the economic growth rate. They have, therefore, concluded that the slow growth of Africa is due to the great degree of ethnicity.

27 These academics include Collier and Hoeffler, Fearon and Laitin, and Miguel.

28 A medical doctor who has worked on the HIV/AIDS pandemic, Peter Mugenyi (2008), writes in his book *Genocide by Denial: How Profiteering from HIV/*

AIDS Killed Millions about the conspiracy theories surrounding HIV/AIDS and how the US does not want to accept it began in that country. He claims that this is what delayed the open public campaign about AIDS in the US.

29 There are still those who have differing views on the origins and causes of AIDS. Referred to as sceptics, they claim that the truth about HIV/AIDS has been suppressed. They include Peter H. Duesberg, a professor of molecular and cell biology at Berkeley, who, in his book *Inventing the Aids Virus*, says that one of the pathogenic factors behind AIDS is malnutrition and parasitic infections (Duesberg, 1996). Robert-Root Bernstein, professor of physiology at Michigan State University, claims that HIV does not play a central role in the onset of AIDS. See www.news.bbc.co.uk/2/hi/Africa/72099.stm (accessed on 23 January 2012).

30 See: http://en.wikipedia.org/wiki/HIV/AIDS_in_South_Africa (accessed on 23 January 2012).

31 See http://www.usaid.gov/our_work/global_health/aids/Countries/africa/swaziland_profilepdf (accessed on 27 January 2012).

32 Cultural influences can make a major difference to work ethics, responsible conduct, spirited motivation, dynamic management, entrepreneurial initiatives, willingness to take risks and a variety of other aspects of human behaviour that can be critical to economic success (Sen, 2004).

33 According to Agrawal et al. (2007), the debate about the savings-growth nexus can be grouped into two leading schools. Firstly, there are the so-called growth theorists, such as Harrod, Domar, Romer and Lucas, who assume that all savings are automatically invested and translated into growth; this means that savings lead to growth. And, secondly, the 'consumption theorists', such as Modigliani, Deaton and Paxson, and Carroll and Weil, who argue that income and its growth determine consumption and, therefore, savings.

34 Jephias Mapuva and Freeman Chari (2010) have questioned the issue of culture, as presented by Huntington (1991). They wonder why Pyongyang is not as advanced as its sister capital, Seoul. If a Korean culture was at play here, they ask, why then is Seoul more advanced than Pyongyang? Were they not the same Korea before the 1950s, or did North Koreans develop new genes after the separation?

35 See http://www.businessweek.com/magazine/content/10_25/b4183010451928.htm (Accessed September 2010).

36 Some experts, such as Professor Nuwagaba, have called on their leaders to practise 'positive dictatorship'. Nuwagaba seems to suggest that for any (de-

veloping country) government to run effectively, there is a need for benevolent leadership. He called on President Museveni of Uganda to exercise positive dictatorship (see *Sunday Monitor*, 22 January 2012).

37 In an opinion survey by a Korean newspaper in April 1997, 75.9 per cent of the respondents selected Park Chung-Hee as the president who had fulfilled his duties best. A mere 3.7 per cent selected President Kim Young Sam, who held office at that time. An opinion poll by the government found Chung-Hee was still held in high esteem. Among the historic personalities of Korea, Park Chung-Hee occupied first place in the esteem of the respondents (at 23.4 per cent) (see Kamppeter, 2008).

38 My discussions with security officials in two of the five East African countries show that during the recruitment process for positions in public agencies and the civil service, behind your back a security screening is done. One of the key issues they screen is whether you and your spouse are members of the ruling party, and who are your friends who call your cellphone. In some cases, more than ethnicity, the sub-ethnic group and one's place of origin are the key determining factors in whether one is successful in the selection process – not competencies. If a candidate has ever received a call from key figures in opposition, even inadvertently, he or she can forget about a job on merit. Brains, qualifications and experience do not matter; political affiliation and connections do. The present author has experienced this process personally.

39 In Canada there are different levels of screening. You can work in government agencies only if you have been security screened at a higher level. However, screening has nothing to do with your political affiliation, your closeness to those families that control power or whether you are distantly related to a former associate of the top leaders, but has now fallen out with the top people.

Committed leadership or multi-party democracy?

1 Statement by the President of the United Republic of Tanzania, His Excellency Benjamin William Mkapa, at the World Bank Conference On Scaling Up Poverty Reduction, Shanghai International Convention Centre, 26 May 2004. Available at http://www.tanzania.go.tz/hotuba/hotuba/040526Hotuba_ya_RaisShanghai.htm (accessed on 16 January 2012).

2 Right from the beginning, Lee Kwan-Yew and his Peoples Progressive Party aggressively promoted industrial development. Industrialisation is a key pillar of economic growth – and jobs, exports and foreign exchange receipts.

3 Quoted in Barro (1999), Huntington: 'The central process of democracy is the selection of leaders through competitive elections by the people they govern . . . The democratic method is that institutional arrangements for arriving at political decisions in which individuals acquire the power to decide by means of a competitive struggle for the people's vote.'

However, many argue democracy is not just about whether many parties exist and compete in a political system, or how many years an elected government survives the system. At heart, it is about the quality of change within political institutions and political cultures. The concern has been that democracy exists in form but not in substance in many countries – the formal institutions such as a political system that is fair, elections and popular sovereignty are there, but democratic preferences, procedures and habits might not have taken root yet. Bui (2010).

4 See http://www.wto.org/english/res_e/statis_e/statis_e.htm (accessed on 14 March 2012).

5 See https://www.uschina.org/public/exports/2000_2010/full_state_report.pdf (accessed on 14 March 2012).

6 Rubén Hernández-Murillo and Christopher J. Martinek, both at the Federal Reserve Bank of St. Louis, published an article: Which came first – democracy or growth? *The Regional Economist*, April 2004. For more on the work of Hernández-Murillo, see http://research.stlouisfed.org/publications/regional/08/04/democracy.pdf (accessed on October 2012).

7 Bush narrowly won the November 7 election, with 271 electoral votes to Gore's 266 (with one elector abstaining in the official tally). The election was noteworthy for a controversy over the awarding of Florida's 25 electoral votes, the subsequent recount process in that state and the unusual event of the winning candidate having received fewer popular votes than the runner-up. It was the closest election since 1876 and only the fourth election in which the electoral vote did not reflect the popular vote. (Source: http://

en.wikipedia.org/wiki/United_States_presidential_election,_2000 [accessed on 14 March 2012]). Also one needs to read the per Curiam decision of the seven with regard to the case: Supreme Court of the United States George W. Bush, et al., petitioners *v.* Albert Gore, Jr., et al. on writ of certiorari to the Florida Supreme Court, 12 December 2000. In this case the respondents complained of over-voting, and non-legal votes. Available at http://www.law.cornell.edu/supct/html/00-949.ZPC.html (accessed on 14 March 2012).

8 In 'Did Dubby rig the election?', published in the *New Statesman*, 29 November 2004, by Michael Meacher, it is claimed that elections could have been rigged in favour of Bush against Robert Kelly. Meacher points to the fact that the use of electronic voting systems and optical scanning devices may have had a significant influence on the result, yet security experts insist that such systems are not secure and not tamper-proof. These electronic voting systems and optical scanning devices were used to count a third of the votes across 37 states. Noting that academics and political analysts were drawing comparisons between areas that used paper ballots and areas that used electronic systems, he asked a rhetorical question: Is it possible that results in the latter were rigged? Details available at http://www.newstatesman.com/200411290018.

9 There is an emerging trend in Africa whereby, after election malpractices have been committed in a country, the supposed winner in an election is invited by the incumbent to share power – and the invitee agrees. This has happened in Kenya and Zimbabwe, and those invited have justified their decision by claiming it creates peace.

10 A professor of constitutional law and former Judge of the African court Justice, Professor George W. Kanyeihamba, once asked how peasants could decide any county's future, noting that many of them were illiterate people whose main preoccupation was cheap but dangerous local brew (known as *enguli*). In some African countries, a vote can be bought for a quarter of a dollar. Source details at: http://www.sunrise.ug.

11 According to Moyo (2009), poor countries with the lowest levels of economic development need decisive and benevolent dictators to push through reforms that are required to ensure that their economies move towards growth and development.

12 See 2006 UNESCO BREDA Sub-Regional Statistics and Analysis North Africa, http://www.poledakar.org/IMG/North_Africa-web.pdf (accessed on 14 March 2012).

13 As mentioned, the success of Singapore, for example, has got a lot to do with Lee Kwan-Yew as an individual leader.

14 This has happened before with regard to the Iranian Revolution of 1979, when the Ayatollah more or less hijacked the ongoing revolution, which had been instigated as a secular movement to get rid of the Shah. As the events unravelled, one despotic ruler was replaced by another, regardless of the motives for the revolution.

15 See Remarks by the President to the Ghanaian Parliament, 11 July 2009, at http://www.america.gov/st/texttrans-english/2009/July/20090711110050a bretnuh0.1079783.html&distid=ucs.

16 Ibid.

17 Mbeki says that the West has often defended its 'violent interventions' on the continent by arguing that they act out of the goodness of their hearts with the objective of bringing 'us, the Africans, the gifts of democracy, good governance, peace and the very lives of millions of Africans who would otherwise have been butchered by the African governments concerned . . . We have now seen what happened in Ivory Coast and Libya last year, in both instances to allow non-African countries, ostensibly mandated by the UN Security Council, and regardless of African opinion, to remove the sitting governments by force and thus effect regime change, in the interest of the Western powers.' See http://www.monitor.co.ug/News/National/-/688334/1310636/-/b1i26yz/-/index.html (accessed on 20 January 2012).

18 See Remarks by the President to the Ghanaian Parliament, July 11 2009 at http://www.america.gov/st/texttrans-english/2009/July/20090711110050a bretnuh0.1079783.html&distid=ucs (accessed on 7 November 2010).

The private sector and managing resources

1 There are differing views on Mugabe's land reforms. Some say that his land giveaways are right, and that he is redressing bad history in his country. There are claims that the UK refused to honour a pledge on the issue of land after Mugabe took over. But one wonders why, if there was a problem to solve, he waited this long.

2 Williamson originally came up with this phrase in 1990 to refer to the lowest common denominator of policy advice being addressed by the Washington-based institutions to Latin American countries. The Washington consensus is currently taken to be synonymous with neo-liberalism and globalisation. See *World Bank Research Observer*, 2000. Washington DC: The International Bank for Reconstruction and Development 15(2): 251–264.

3 Liberalisation is the removal of government interference in financial markets, capital markets, and barriers to trade (see Stiglitz, 2002: 59).

4 There are conspiracy theories that the British colonialists knew a long time ago about the presence of oil in Uganda but did not reveal it to the independence government. Obote knew about it, but failed to get support from the British with regard to exploiting it.

5 At the time of writing, African cooperation has failed to contain the problems in Libya. Even the May 2011 meeting to discuss the future of Libya, like the Berlin Conference, which partitioned Africa, took place in London without the participation of the African Union.

6 See http://www.monitor.co.ug/News/National/-/688334/1310636/-/b1i26yz/-/index.html (accessed on 30 January 2012).

7 Mbeki said the West has often defended its 'violent interventions' in Africa by arguing that the West acts out of the goodness of its heart with the objective 'to bring us, the Africans, the gifts of democracy, good governance, peace and the very lives of millions of Africans who would otherwise have been butchered by the African governments concerned ... We have now seen what happened in Ivory Coast and Libya last year, in both instances to allow non-African countries, ostensibly mandated by the UN Security Council, and regardless of African opinion, to remove the sitting governments by force and thus effect regime change, in the interest of the Western powers.' Mbeki added that an apparent lack of continental cohesion had done little to fend off the ability of the post-modern world to achieve the dominance it seeks in Africa. A NATO-led offensive in Libya toppled Muammar Gaddafi in August 2011 before his brutal death two months later, while a French-sponsored onslaught in Ivory Coast led to the overthrow of Laurent Gbagbo in

April 2011, despite AU intercessions for internal solutions to the political crises in both countries. See http://www.monitor.co.ug/News/National/-/688334/1310636/-/b1i26yz/-/index.html (accessed on 30 January 2012).

8 Steve Biko was the visionary leader of the Black Consciousness Movement during the apartheid era in South Africa. Biko referred to 'black' as a situation of oppression. So, for Biko, the word 'black' did not refer to skin colour. If you were black, coloured, Indian or white and felt oppressed, you were black.

9 This observation is based on the author's discussions with Africans living in Africa, Europe and the US.

Effect of corruption on economic growth and development

1 The author was told the following story by a Zairian (whether it was true or not is unknown): at one of his meetings with the donors at the Paris Club, Mobutu was asked: 'Mr President, you have enough money, why don't you lend to your county, Zaire?' Mobutu replied: 'No. I don't trust the Zairians.'

2 The cost of corruption in Africa, BBC News, 17 February 2006. Corruption costs African countries an estimated 25 per cent of their combined national income – some $148 billion a year. See also BBC, 13 October 2004, Africans let down by governments – results of a BBC survey on corruption. Fifty-four African families were polled for the report, which covers 28 of the continent's 53 countries, http://news.bbc.co.uk/2/hi/africa/3736956.stm (accessed on 9 July 2010).

3 In Uganda in 2009, the chief executive of the National Forestry Authority stole the equivalent of $450 000. He was later interdicted and is facing the law on issues of abuse of office (i.e. corruption).

4 An example of extreme retributive justice is the sort applied in Arab countries, such as cutting off thieves' hands. And during his era in Uganda, Amin put an end to robbery by authorising the police and military to shoot thieves caught in the act. Despite whatever else is said of Amin, these measures helped deter petty theft while he was president.

5 I am not a revisionist or cultural relativist, as Daniel Kaufmann calls it: those who see corruption with a cultural lens – saying that corruption is viewed differently in developed and less developed countries; or those who see it having a good side of enhancing competition and timely service delivery – even saying that Asian tigers have both phenomenal growth and high levels of corruption. I do not claim there is no corruption in other parts of the world, including the wealthy nations. I acknowledge that there is corruption in the US and Europe. However, my point is that one should insist on fighting corruption in Africa, in particular because those who perpetrate it steal from the poor (and even the poorest of the poor by stealing their aid). And in Africa corruption is rampant – it causes loss of life and undermines basic services. This is not the case with corruption in the developed world. (Daniel Kaufmann, an expert on corruption issues, is a senior fellow at the Brookings Institution and previously director at the World Bank Institute, leading the work on governance and anti-corruption from 2003 until 2008.)

Population strategies and educating the people

1 The demographic dividend occurs when a falling birth rate changes the age distribution in a country, which results in less expenditure and investment to meet the needs of the youngest age groups, and resources are consequently released for investment in economic development and family welfare.

2 It is estimated that the demographic dividend accounted for one-third of East Asia's economic miracle (Bloom & Williamson, 1998; Bloom, Canning & Malaney, 2000).

3 This was the spirit of the Millennium Development Goal Universal Primary Education, agreed by the members of the UN in 2000.

4 See http://www.bea.gov/newsreleases/national/gdp/2012/pdf/gdp4q11_3rd.pdf (accessed on 30 March 2012).

5 US Census Bureau, 2010. Special Edition 2010 Census and Apportionment, http://www.census.gov/newsroom/releases/archives/facts_for_features_special_editions/cb10-ffse05.html (accessed on 30 March 2012).

6 More details from: Wang Feng (2005). Can China afford to continue its one-child policy? *Asia Pacific Issue, Analysis from the East-West Center* 77, March.

7 There were tight social controls limiting who one could marry and at what age, which left a large number of unmarried women in the reproductive age group. It is believed that infanticide and abortion were widely practised in Japan during this period, referred to as *Tokugawa* (see Hanley, S.B., http://www.ncbi.nlm.nih.gov/pubmed/12339409 [accessed on 23 September 2011]).

8 Michael Fairbanks has worked in development in Latin America and Africa. He is the founding member of Seven (Social Equity Venture Fund) – a virtual non-profit entity run by entrepreneurs, whose strategy is to markedly increase the rate of innovation and diffusion of enterprise-based solutions to poverty. He has written and popularised the seven forms of capital: natural endowments (e.g. location, sub-soil assets, forests, beaches and climate); financial resources of a nation (savings and international reserves); institutional capital (legal protection of tangible and intangible property, etc.); human-made capital (buildings, bridges, roads); knowledge resources (international patents, university and think tank capacities); human capital (skills, insights, capabilities); and cultural capital (music, language and ritualistic tradition, attitudes, beliefs and values that are linked to innovation). With Stace Lindsay, Fairbanks co-wrote *Plowing the sea: Nurturing the hidden sources of growth in the developing countries*, which analyses the challenges of competitiveness in developing countries, especially Africa and the Andean region.

9 The MDGs are a set of goals that UN member-country leaders signed up to as a tool to end poverty and illiteracy in developing countries.

10 John Bongaarts (1998) of the Population Council, New York, defines the dependency burden as the ratio of dependent young and old to the proportion of the population of working age.

11 This is not to imply that all countries have to realise higher levels of growth only via industrialisation. With political stability, peace and security, some countries in sub-Saharan Africa can grow by attracting tourism and increased involvement in ICT, for example.

The informal sector and tools for attracting investment

1 Informality in an economy means different things to different people, but mostly bad things, such as unprotected workers, excessive regulation, low productivity, unfair competition, evasion of the rule of law, underpayment or non-payment of taxes, and working 'underground' or in the 'shadows' (see World Bank: *The informal sector: What is it, why do we care, and how do we measure it?* At http://siteresources.worldbank.org/INTLAC/Resources/CH1.pdf (accessed on 30 August 2011); see also Fiess et al., 2006.

2 In Becker's study published by SIDA (2004), the results of a household survey on the overall profile of the informal sector in Tanzania estimated that 34 per cent of total households in mainland Tanzania are engaged in informal-sector activities at any given point of time. The proportion in urban areas was much higher, with a peak of 55 per cent of households in Dar es Salaam engaged in the informal sector.

3 In this study, almost all the sub-Saharan countries were surveyed.

4 The ILO (2002) defines the informal economy by categorising those who work in the informal sector as grouped into some basic employment categories – 1) Employer: owners of informal enterprises; owner operators of informal enterprises; 2) Self-employed: own-account workers; heads of family businesses; and unpaid family workers; and 3) Wage workers: employees of informal enterprises; casual workers without a fixed employer; home workers (also called industrial outworkers); domestic workers; temporary and part-time workers; unregistered workers.

5 The ILO (2002) has put forward another view, a more optimistic scenario about the existence of the informal sector, that of 'growth from below'. This view asserts that in some regions, countries or industries, the small-business and micro-business sectors are more dynamic and create more jobs than the formal sector.

6 The middle class should not be just a politically created middle class propped up by a political system. This can easily disappear with the fall of the political system that created it.

7 See the *Economist*, 12 February 2009. 'A special report on the new middle classes in emerging markets', http://www.economist.com/node/13063298 (accessed on 24 October 2010).

8 Quoted in the *Economist* (http://www.economist.com/node/13063298) (accessed on 24 October 2010). Diana Farrell of the America's National Economic Council, who formerly worked for McKinsey, a consultancy, defines the middle classes at roughly starting from the point where people have one-

third of their income left for discretionary spending after providing for basic food and shelter. This level of income allows them to buy goods for the home and afford family healthcare and education for their children.

9   Homi Kharas argues that the 'sweet spot of growth', the point at which the poor start entering the middle class, is the moment when poor countries can get the maximum benefit from their cheap labour through international trade, before they price themselves out of world markets for cheap goods or are able to compete with rich countries in making high-value goods. Kharas also adds that it is almost always a period of fast urbanisation, when formerly underemployed farmers abandon rural life for the cities to work in manufacturing. Eventually this results in a lessening of income inequalities because the new middle class sits somewhere between the rich elite and the rural poor. See the *Economist*, http://www.economist.com/node/13063298 (accessed).

10 This led the US to support some of the worst African dictators, who looted their countries, such as Mobutu of Zaire.

11 Moyo (2009) says that aid has not benefited Africa's economic growth, and that instead it has stifled it.

12 Rwanda's Kagame has done this. He stripped officials of their four-wheel-drive vehicles and sold them.

13 Cyril Chami, Tanzania's minister for industry and trade, has said such foreign business persons who have been granted work permit class 'A' but instead embark on conducting small businesses supposedly to have been done by local business persons face several penalties, including deportation. The minister promised that the ministry will centralise requirements needed for doing business, including licences. For more on the decision to flush out bogus foreign investors in Tanzania, visit http://www.dailynews.co.tz/home/?n = 15624 (accessed on 10 October 2011).

14 According to the joint report 2010 by the World Bank and African Development Bank, only about half of sub-Saharan African countries reported remittance data with any regularity. Some countries, such as the Central African Republic, the DRC, Somalia and Zimbabwe – all of which are believed to receive significant remittance flows – reported no remittance data. The report also shows that in this region, cross-border flows via such institutions as post offices, savings cooperatives, microfinance institutions and mobile money transfer services are not captured.

15 There are arguments that migration of Africans to developed countries causes a so-called brain drain. However, economics shows that human capital will

go where there is demand for it and it can be handsomely rewarded. Without interference, the market is a good distributor of private goods and services, at a price agreed between the two parties. Therefore, migration cannot be stopped.

16 Let us take the example of Uganda. According to the Bank of Uganda, the country received $980.9 million, which is slightly more than the government's national budget allocated to Uganda's national roads authority in 2009/10 and 2010/11.

17 The author's personal interviews with Ugandans and Kenyans in the diaspora (mainly in the UK, US, Canada and Germany) confirmed that even relatives of expatriates received money and did not buy the items (e.g. property, land) requested by their kin.

18 It is alleged that one of the reasons that foreign currencies appreciated in Uganda during the period after the 2011 elections is because foreign investors repatriated their earnings and banked them in their home countries. This reduced forex in the economy – and this raised the price (i.e. exchange rate) of these currencies.

19 For example, the government of Uganda through the central bank established export refinances schemes to help boost the export sector.

20 The high transaction costs mean that MFIs tend to operate in urban and semi-urban areas, which make it hard to reach the rural communities who are engaged in agriculture, the mainstay of most people in rural areas of the region.

21 The francophone countries it serves include Burkina Faso, Benin, Côte d'Ivoire, Guinea Bissau, Mali, Niger, Senegal and Togo.

22 For more details about depth and liquidity of African stock markets, see Allen, Otchere & Senbet (2010).

23 A survey carried out by Finscope Uganda in 2009 indicated that due to low financial literacy levels, only 21 per cent of Ugandans use banks; 7 per cent access financial services formally; 42 per cent are informally served; and 30 per cent are financially excluded. See http://www.newvision.co.ug/D/8/220/745644 (accessed on 15 October 2011).

24 Milton Friedman, a protégé of the Chicago School and a leading monetarist, was awarded the Nobel Prize in Economics in 1976 and served as advisor to Presidents Nixon and Reagan. Details of Milton Friedman's views on free markets and property rights can be found in his book *Capitalism and Freedom* (Friedman, 1962); see also the following in an interview at: http://www.pbs.org/wgbh/commandingheights/shared/pdf/int_miltonfriedman.pdf (accessed on 6 November 2011).

Regional and international trade relations

1 ECOWAS was one of the earliest regional groups in Africa. Comprising 15 member countries, it was founded on 28 May 1975, with the signing of the Treaty of Lagos.

2 There is the argument that because of the levels of debt and financial woes in Greece, Italy, Spain and Ireland, their people would not agree with this sentiment. We have to note, however, that countries require prudence and living within their means, whether under a political or economic federation. The benefits of a higher level of integration outweigh the possible challenges of the union.

3 Only eight of the RECs are officially recognised by the African Economic Community (AEC). The AEC is an organisation of African Union states establishing grounds for mutual economic development among the majority of African states: creation of free trade areas, customs unions, a single market, a central bank, a common currency, and ultimately establishing an economic and monetary union. The eight RECs are CEN-SAD, SADC, COMESA, EAC, AMU, ECCAS, ECOWAS and IGAD.

4 According to the *Boston Globe*, the US government has confirmed that Taylor worked with US spy agencies during his rise as one of the world's most notorious dictators. See http://articles.boston.com/2012-01-17/metro/30632769_1_courtenay-griffiths-charles-taylor-war-crimes (accessed on 24 January 2012).

5 President George Bush, after his visit to the continent, gave a big boost to Africa in its fight against HIV/AIDS under the Presidential Fund on AIDS for Africa. President Obama has since endorsed the continuity of this fund.

6 These countries are Angola, Benin, Botswana, Burkina Faso, Burundi, Cameroon, Cape Verde, Chad, Comoros, Republic of Congo, DRC, Djibouti, Ethiopia, Gabon, The Gambia, Ghana, Guinea, Guinea-Bissau, Kenya, Lesotho, Liberia, Madagascar, Malawi, Mali, Mauritius, Mozambique, Namibia, Niger, Nigeria, Rwanda, São Tomé and Príncipe, Senegal, Seychelles, Sierra Leone, South Africa, Swaziland, Tanzania, Togo, Uganda and Zambia (Source: http://www.agoa.gov/eligibility/country_eligibility.html (accessed on 14 December 2011).

7 Working on trade promotion for Uganda, the author remembers that for a long time the Mauritian embassy in the US had staff working and lobbying for such an opportunity. The person lobbying in the 1990s, Peter Craig, was an advisor to the prime minister and an employee of the Mauritius Export Development and Investment Authority (MEDIA).

8 The *Economist*, http://www.economist.com/node/18651512 (accessed on 15 January 2012).

9 This average is after one has discounted the year 2008 when the Industrial and Commercial Bank of China purchased a 20 per cent stake of South Africa's Standard Bank for around $5 billion.

10 Deborah Brautigam's Testimony on China's Growing Role in Africa before the United States Senate Committee on Foreign Relations Subcommittee on African Affairs. Her testimony draws on her books *The Dragon's Gift: The Real Story of China in Africa* and *China in Africa: What Can Western Donors Learn?* Brautigam is a professor at the School of International Service, American University, Washington, DC and senior research fellow, International Food Policy Research Institute. See http://www.foreign.senate.gov/imo/media/doc/Deborah_Brautigam_Testimony.pdf (accessed on 10 January 2012).

11 See http://english.mofcom.gov.cn/statistic/statistic.html (accessed on 29 January 2012).

12 Details for the China-Africa Strategy and the China–Africa forum (FOCAC, November 2006): http:// www. focac.org/eng/ (accessed on 26 January 2012).

13 According to non-governmental organisations, such as Save Darfur and the Peace Research Institute Oslo, China is the supplier of arms to the government of Sudan, has sold arms and weapons to Sudan since the 1990s and has helped establish weapons factories in Sudan. (See The Sudan Referendum and Neighbouring Countries: Egypt and Uganda, Peace Research Institute Oslo, 2010.)

14 The European Centre for Development and Programme Management has published a discussion paper titled *Shopping for Raw Materials: Should Africa be Worried about the EU Raw Materials Initiative?* The publication gives details of available minerals in Africa and possible interests from the EU, China and the US. See www.ecdpm.org/dp105 (accessed on 18 December 2012).

15 Some countries have already paid dearly in the support effort to fight global terror in Africa. More than 70 people were killed in Uganda on July 11 2010, when watching a Soccer World Cup telecast from South Africa. Before that, terrorists bombed US embassies in Tanzania and Kenya. These atrocities show how integrated the world is and the need to work together.

Access to markets and 'just and fair' trade

1 Evidence is available from the WTO.

2 It was surprising at the 2005 WTO ministerial conference in Hong Kong to see the high-level manoeuvres of powerful countries when meeting the developing countries. The US delegation, headed by Robert B. Zoellick, then chief trade negotiator and the current president of the World Bank, announced that they had given more support to AGOA beneficiaries (about $200 million). The author remembers asking some African and US delegates, why this generosity now?

3 This was the gist of Elly Twineyo-Kamugisha's presentation *Issues for Clarification under the EAC-EC-EPA Negotiations* at the Joint EAC-EC-EPA Sensitization Workshop, Dar es Salaam, 8 June 2010. 'What has been done to ensure that EAC countries do benefit from trading under the non-reciprocal arrangement? We hope that the principle of asymmetry will help to ensure that both the EAC and the EU have a trade and development relationship that is mutually beneficial to the parties.'

4 As Kwame Nkrumah said, Africans should face forward: 'We face neither North nor South: We face forward.' *African Journal of Environmental Science and Technology* 3(10), http://www.academicjournals.org/AJest/PDF/pdf%202009/Oct/AJEST-%20Editorial%20-%20October.pdf (accessed on 14 January 2012).

5 Economic diplomacy has been defined by Ambassador Amolo as 'getting a larger share of the world economic cake for your country and people'.

Are international NGOs promoting Africa's economic growth?

1 Find out who runs the show in the world's weakest states with a list of the world's most powerful NGOs at www.ForeignPolicy.com/extras/newcolonialists.

2 Michael A. Cohen, Maria Figueroa Küpçü and Parag Khanna are senior research fellows at the New America Foundation (The article was published in the Foreign Policy magazine of . June 16, 2008)

3 The World Bank (in its Operational Directive 14.70) states that NGOs can be private organisations 'characterized primarily by humanitarian or cooperative, rather than commercial, objectives ... that pursue activities to relieve suffering, promote the interests of the poor, protect the environment, provide basic social services, or undertake community development' working in developing countries. Most of them are based in the developed world; others are locally based organisations (these are usually not financially strong). I will use this definition (other writers exclude CBOs from this definition), to apply to all non-governmental sector organisations. In developing countries you can't separate CBOs and local NGOs because they all have members and do the same work, though at different levels.

4 According to Werker and Ahmed (2008), NGOs are frequently idealised as organisations committed to 'doing good', while setting aside profit or politics (see Zivetz, 1991; Fisher, 1997). In the realm of international development, NGOs have been characterised as the new 'favoured child' of official development agencies and proclaimed as a 'magic bullet' to target and fix the problems that have befallen the development process (see Hulme & Edwards, 1997).

5 Barr, Fafchamps and Owens (2005) surveyed the Ugandan NGO sector in depth. They carried out a representative sample of 199 of the 3 159 registered NGOs. The vast majority of them have very little revenue. Four large international NGOs from their 199 responses accounted for well over half of the revenue. While the average revenue per NGO is $274 000, the median is only $22 000. Most funding from outside sources (international NGOs and bilateral donors) is allocated to these large NGOs, while small NGOs depend more heavily for their budget – over 50 per cent – on membership fees, local fundraising and income derived from 'another business'.

6 Mbeki said, 'all of us know . . . that a lot of . . . NGOs, civil-society organisations on the continent are financed from outside the continent'. Implying that their agenda was externally influenced by the objectives of funding sources. President Mbeki made the comments at Makerere University Institute of Social Research, where he was a guest speaker. See *Sunday Monitor*, 22 January 2012, www.monitor.co.ug (accessed on 24 January 2012).

7 See BBC News, 'UK spied on Russians with fake rock', http://www.bbc.co.uk/
   news/world-europe-16614209 (accessed on 21 January 2012).

8 According to Duflo and Kremer (2003), not all the randomised evaluations of
   NGO programmes have found positive outcomes. Some evaluations found no
   difference. Also, a survey by the OECD on the impact and methods of NGOs
   found that 'there is still a lack of firm and reliable evidence on the impact of
   NGO development projects and programmes'. See http://www.valt.helsinki.fi/
   ids/ngo/ (accessed June 2011).

9 When the government of Uganda amended the NGO Registration Act and
   required annual application to the NGO Registration Board, the NGO frater-
   nity opposed it. They petitioned the president. They went to court. There are
   several reasons why they opposed this law. It would limit their political or
   civil society's space. It would also require time to prepare the annual application. The government is trying to limit freedoms and curtail the rights of civil
   society. And they are the representatives of the common person, the poor, the
   vulnerable and the voiceless.

10 This is not limited to Africa. Kendall Stiles (2002) has argued that the growth
   and sophistication of Bangladesh's NGO sector may cause some of these
   organisations to seek a greater presence in the public arena by getting involved in politics.

11 See European charities 'want Africa to remain poor', at http://www.africareview.
   com/News/European + aid + agencies + want + a + poor + Africa/-/979180/
   1372652/-/qtue5mz/-/index.html (accessed on 12 April 2012).

12 INGO management and their so-called experts live as men and women of
   means. Every manager of these INGOs is bought a new vehicle, comprehen-
   sively insured, and given solar power in addition to grid power, and accom-
   modated in luxurious housing. In the evenings they will wine and dine with
   the VIPS. Even when these INGOs find the local staff of these organisations
   walking on foot to deliver services to the people, they will never give them
   rides in their vehicles. There are rules of getting a ride on these vehicles.

13 Most trade campaigners are calling on the rich countries to open up their
   markets to the goods from developing countries. They say that when they
   were developing, developed countries used protections. Now they want the
   developing countries to remove protections before they have developed. This
   is presented well by Professor Ha-Joon Chang (2002).